HERMANN AND DOROTHEA

JOHANN WOLFGANG VON
GOETHE

Hermann and Dorothea

Translated, with an introduction, by
DANIEL COOGAN
Professor of German
Brooklyn College
The City University of New York

FREDERICK UNGAR PUBLISHING CO.
NEW YORK

Second Printing, 1976

Printed in the United States of America

Library of Congress Catalog Card No. 66-21737

ISBN 0-8044-6188-0

Dedicated
with grateful affection
to

SAMUEL HART NEWHALL

cui tanta debeo

INTRODUCTION

After he had completed *Wilhelm Meisters Lehrjahre* in 1796 Goethe sought a literary task of smaller compass and different in form. Thirteen years before, the German translator of Homer, Johann Heinrich Voss, had published a charming rustic epic, *Luise,* in dactylic hexameters, which had evoked Goethe's admiration. Goethe himself had employed the hexameter in his political allegory *Reineke Fuchs* (1793), but this work had met with little popularity. Believing, however, that this metric form, which had also been used by the great Klopstock in his *Messias* (1748 ff.), was well suited to the German language, Goethe was determined to use it again. He found a suitable subject in the account of the wanderings of some Protestant exiles from Salzburg, which he read in 1794.* In this account was the following anecdote, which became the basis for Goethe's plot.

The son of a rich man asks a girl in the group of refugees whether she is willing to serve in his father's house. She declares her willingness, whereupon the son goes to his father, who has long been urging him to marry, and delivers an ultimatum: he will either marry this girl or no one at all. His father, the minister, and other friends of the family at first advise him against such an unpromising union, but finally, seeing his earnestness, acquiesce. The young man then presents the girl to them, without telling her of his matrimonial intentions. The father asks her if she will accept his son in marriage, to which she reacts by taking offense. When, however, the young man explains himself to her, she joyfully accedes to his proposal and produces a purse containing a dowry of two hundred ducats.

* Göcking, *Das liebtätige Gera gegen die Salzburgischen Emigranten.*

In adapting this story, Goethe advanced the period to that of his own day; in his poem, the exiles are fleeing from the terrors of the French Revolution. He himself had at first welcomed the Revolution, but later came to reject it because of its violent excesses. It has been suggested also that certain information of a personal nature, which came to him about the time he began to write his poem, had a determining influence upon it. This information concerned the woman to whom he had once been engaged: Frau Elisabeth von Türckheim, better known as Lili Schönemann, the Frankfurt beauty who had inspired some of his noblest poetry twenty years before.

Lili had married and lived with her husband and five children in great prosperity in the French city of Straßburg, of which Herr von Türckheim was mayor, until the coming of the Revolution. Türckheim's prestige and prosperity drew the attention of the revolutionary authorities, who eventually ousted him from office and forbade him to enter the city. In July, 1794, an order was issued for his arrest. He was able to escape to the German border, but was compelled to leave his wife and children behind. Subsequently his wife disguised herself as a farm woman and, carrying her youngest child on her back, walked with the other four to the German border, successfully negotiated its crossing, and continued her journey to Heidelberg. News of her heroic exploit reached Goethe in 1795, and this, coupled with other information, refreshed his memory of her.

Goethe's biographer, Albert Bielschowsky, regards this episode as the decisive impetus in the shaping of Goethe's little epic; he believes it to be the personal experience which makes *Hermann und Dorothea,* like all Goethe's works, a "fragment of a great confession." Though it has some support, not all biographers and literary critics share Bielschowsky's opinion.

Hermann und Dorothea was published in 1797, having been written within the space of a single year. Next to *Faust* and *Wilhelm Meister,* it has remained ever since the most loved masterpiece of Germany's greatest poet. It was also Goethe's favorite among his writings and, as late as 1825, he said to Eckermann that it was almost the only one of his longer poems which he enjoyed rereading. He never could read it, he said, without emotion. He added that he most enjoyed reading it in its Latin translation.

Although the poem was not at first received warmly by the general public, it found immediate acclaim from such critics as Schiller, who immediately wrote Goethe of the emotion he felt upon reading it, and concluding by saying that "it is perfect in its genre—moving in its pathos and charming to the highest degree—in short, beautiful. . . ." * In another passage Schiller expresses his envy of Goethe's ability to write such a poem: all he need do, he said, was shake the tree of poetry and the most delicious fruit would fall to the ground.

Despite the speed of composition, Goethe exercised great care in constructing the poem. The choice of names for the titular figures, for example, is far from accidental. The juxtaposition of the Teutonic Hermann with the Greek Dorothea fortifies Goethe's purpose: to establish a firm connection between contemporary German literature and the heritage of classical antiquity. The same purpose is indicated, of course, in the choice of the Homeric hexameter as the vehicle for a simple contemporary German story. Nor is the superscription of each of the nine cantos a random choice. The names of the Muses are chosen with deliberation. Thus the name of the Muse of Comedy, Thalia, heads the canto (III) subtitled "The Citizens," in which the only character who verges on the comic, the druggist, is permitted his fullest say. Similarly Clio, the Muse of History, presides over "The Times" (Canto VI), while Urania, the Muse of Astronomy, gives her name and celestial lustre to the "Prospect" (Canto IX), with which the epic closes.

Equally significant is Goethe's alteration of the motivation of the emigration from religious to political. He was more interested in the vast canvas of political upheaval than in the petty interde-

* Schiller, letter to Goethe, October 20, 1797.

nominational squabble which underlay the events described in Göcking's account. In Goethe's own words: "I have sought to reflect the great movements on the stage of the world in a small mirror." *

The highest poetic level of the epic is probably achieved in the scenes between mother and son in Canto IV, and between the lovers in Canto VIII. In the former there is perhaps a reflection of Goethe's relationship with his own mother, who shortly before the publication of the work expressed her delighted anticipation of a "poem, in which a Frau Aja [her own nickname] is supposed to occur." In his description of the wonderfully delicate, warm, loving relationship between the two young people in Canto VIII, Goethe achieves a mastery which he seldom if ever equalled.

Together with *Torquato Tasso* and *Iphigenie auf Tauris, Hermann und Dorothea* belongs to those of Goethe's works which most deeply concern themselves with humanity—"*Alle menschlichen Gebrechen sühnet reine Menschlichkeit.*" (Pure humanity heals all human failings.) Against the distant background of war and national upheaval, against the clear foreground of a simple German city in a simple but beautiful German countryside, it is the half-dozen human beings who occupy our attention and arouse our feelings. Let us take a closer look at them.

The druggist is a representative of the past, a conservative *laudator temporis acti,* preferring the graceful curlicues of the rococo to the stark simplicity of "modern" style. He is miserly, tactless, selfish, content to live by and for himself, yet terribly curious about others' affairs. He is garrulous and opinionated, but not without a certain shrewdness.

The innkeeper, Hermann's father, is more admirable than the druggist, though like him he is inclined to be selfish. His gruffness conceals a soft heart, and despite his momentary unkindness to Hermann he is a devoted husband and father. He is somewhat pretentious and boastful; he regards himself as a man of the times, taking pride in the achievements of his own generation, and

* Letter to J. H. Meyer, June, 1796.

much gratified by his own participation in civic affairs. His ambition for his only child is that Hermann will be even more successful—in a worldly sense—than he himself has been.

The pastor is the figure of conciliation: between the old and the new, the secular and the religious, the father and the son, the man and the woman. He has a deep, inspiring faith in the goodness of God and of His creation, particularly man. There is no indication of confessional identity; all references which might indicate his denomination are avoided. He is wise and intuitive, learned, intelligent, persuasive, eloquent. One wonders, especially after hearing his reminiscence of his sojourn in Straßburg, whether Goethe had not in mind Johann Gottfried Herder (1744–1803), who was also a clergyman, and who had befriended and inspired Goethe in Straßburg in 1770 and 1771.

Hermann's mother is a wise, kind woman firmly attached to the good earth and its gifts. She takes great joy in her work, her possessions, and above all her family, particularly her son, whom she loves with understanding and compassion. It is a delicate touch that the full beauty of the landscape setting of the epic is revealed as Goethe introduces us to her most fully, as if she were extremely close to nature, to its goodness and truth. She ends her search for Hermann at the foot of the great tree which, like her, dispenses shade and refreshment to those who seek them. Her conversation there with Hermann marks the turning point in the young man's life, which is made worthy and meaningful because of the love and truth which she manifests in her counsel to him.

Of all the characters, it is Hermann alone who passes through some kind of self-development; the others are fully formed at the beginning. His perfecting comes about through his association with and commitment to Dorothea. He is slow, careful, honest, a bit stodgy, perhaps, and quite unable to cope with ultrasophistication or façade. He can neither understand nor be interested in ephemeral fashions; rather he shows interest only in that which is timeless and eternally valid—his work on the land, his family, his beloved.

Dorothea is the agent through whom Hermann matures. As his love for her stirs within him, his true nobility and worth become apparent. In the end he has won the respect and admiration even of his father, who at first was so dissatisfied with his son.

Dorothea is described less fully than the others. She is free, independent, strong. A single incident from her past is enough to convince us of her heroic capabilities. Goethe is careful to describe her in more *physical* detail (twice) than he employs for any other character, but her role in the epic would have been hampered had he given us too close an account of her origins, her parents, and her personality. He chooses rather to let us judge the total person by her effect on others.

At the close of the epic the characters are brought together for the first and only time, and the behavior of each is consistent with the part he or she has previously played. The work ends on a positive and optimistic note.

In 1798, in a long essay on *Hermann und Dorothea,* a great literary critic and philologist, Wilhelm von Humboldt (1767-1835), who was one of the founders of the University of Berlin and a great friend of Goethe, wrote as follows:

> The plain simplicity of the subject described, and the depth and grandeur of the effects produced by this description most strongly and irresistibly move the reader to admire Goethe's *Hermann und Dorothea*. . . . The poet has understood very well how to depict humanity in its progress, brought about by its own inner strength and by outside impetus. He has given this material a higher ideal poetic quality by selecting for his characters persons who have not been spoiled by too much civilization but are not immune to civilizing influences. His principals have something about them which reminds us of the heroes of Homer. He has given his subject matter more vivid life by showing all the special qualities of our national character and our period of history.

> . . . With special skill our poet has erected a beautiful and touching monument to the creative power of woman.

This contemporary evaluation of Goethe's *Hermann und Dorothea* is echoed in the judgment of critics—and audiences—of our own time.

D. C.

HERMANN AND DOROTHEA

I

KALLIOPE

Schicksal und Anteil

Hab ich den Markt und die Straßen doch nie so einsam gesehen!
Ist doch die Stadt wie gekehrt! wie ausgestorben! Nicht funfzig,
Deucht mir, blieben zurück, von allen unsern Bewohnern.
Was die Neugier nicht tut! So rennt und läuft nun ein jeder,
Um den traurigen Zug der armen Vertriebnen zu sehen.
Bis zum Dammweg, welchen sie ziehn, ist's immer ein Stündchen,
Und da läuft man hinab, im heißen Staube des Mittags.
Möcht ich mich doch nicht rühren vom Platz, um zu sehen das Elend
Guter fliehender Menschen, die nun, mit geretteter Habe,
Leider, das überrheinische Land, das schöne, verlassend,
Zu uns herüber kommen, und durch den glücklichen Winkel
Dieses fruchtbaren Tals und seiner Krümmungen wandern.
Trefflich hast du gehandelt, o Frau, daß du milde den Sohn fort
Schicktest, mit altem Linnen und etwas Essen und Trinken,
Um es den Armen zu spenden; denn Geben ist Sache des Reichen.
Was der Junge doch fährt! und wie er bändigt die Hengste!
Sehr gut nimmt das Kütschchen sich aus, das neue; bequemlich
Säßen viere darin, und auf dem Bocke der Kutscher.
Diesmal fuhr er allein; wie rollt es leicht um die Ecke!
So sprach, unter dem Tore des Hauses sitzend am Markte,
Wohlbehaglich, zur Frau der Wirt zum Goldenen Löwen.

I

CALLIOPE

Fate and Sympathy

"Never yet have I seen the market and streets so deserted!
Why, the city appears to be swept and empty of people!
Not even fifty of all our townsmen, I think, have remained here.
Curiosity makes them come running, now, to behold how
Slowly and sadly the miserable exiles move past our city.
One hour's travel is needed down to the highway they're taking,
Yet they were eager to go, in the heat and the dust of the
noontime.
I would not move from this spot to witness the woe of the
wand'rers,
Who, with what they could save, poor souls, are fleeing their
country,
Leaving their beautiful land on the Rhine River's other embankment, 10
Crossing over to us, and traversing our fortunate region,
Wending their way through the length of our fruitful,
meandering valley.
Wisely and well have you acted, my dear, in kindly despatching
Hermann, our son, to the exiles, laden with clothing and food and
Good things to drink, to strengthen their bodies and lighten
their troubles.
Giving is only the wealthy man's duty. Just see how our youngster
Drives those powerful stallions, and look how handsome the
coach is!
New, with space for four, and room on the box for the coachman.
Now he is driving alone; how smoothly he rolls round the corner!"
Thus, as he sat by the gate of his stately abode near the market, 20
Spoke to his wife, with great relish, the host of the
Gold-painted Lion.

Und es versetzte darauf die kluge verständige Hausfrau:
Vater, nicht gerne verschenk ich die abgetragene Leinwand;
Denn sie ist zu manchem Gebrauch und für Geld nicht zu haben,
Wenn man ihrer bedarf. Doch heute gab ich so gerne
Manches bessere Stück an Überzügen und Hemden;
Denn ich hörte von Kindern und Alten, die nackend daher gehn.
Wirst du mir aber verzeihn? denn auch dein Schrank ist geplündert.
Und besonders den Schlafrock mit indianischen Blumen,
Von dem feinsten Kattun, mit feinem Flanelle gefüttert,
Gab ich hin; er ist dünn und alt und ganz aus der Mode.

Aber es lächelte drauf der treffliche Hauswirt und sagte:
Ungern vermiß ich ihn doch, den alten kattunenen Schlafrock,
Echt ostindischen Stoffs; so etwas kriegt man nicht wieder.
Wohl! ich trug ihn nicht mehr. Man will jetzt freilich, der Mann soll
Immer gehn im Surtout und in der Pekesche sich zeigen,
Immer gestiefelt sein; verbannt ist Pantoffel und Mütze.

Siehe! versetzte die Frau, dort kommen schon einige wieder,
Die den Zug mit gesehn; er muß doch wohl schon vorbei sein.
Seht, wie allen die Schuhe so staubig sind! wie die Gesichter
Glühen! und jeglicher führt das Schnupftuch, und wischt sich den Schweiß ab.
Möcht ich doch auch, in der Hitze, nach solchem Schauspiel so weit nicht
Laufen und leiden! Fürwahr, ich habe genug am Erzählten.

Und es sagte darauf der gute Vater mit Nachdruck:
Solch ein Wetter ist selten zu solcher Ernte gekommen,

To him spoke in her turn his discerning, intelligent helpmeet:
"Father, I am not always inclined to dispose of old linen.
Many the time I might use it, and money never can
buy it
Just at the moment of need. But today I had no misgivings:
Excellent bedclothes and shirts I cheerfully, willingly offered,
When I heard of children and old folks who have no more
clothing.
Can you forgive me? I plundered your closet also.
Your pardon!
Even your favorite housecoat I took, with the Indian flowers,
Made of the very best cotton, and lined with quality flannel. 30
You cannot wear it again: it is thin, and gone out of fashion."

Then the excellent publican smiled and replied to his helpmeet:
"Truly I'll sorely be missing my old cotton housecoat
in future:
Real East Indian cloth—I'll never get one just like it.
Well—I hadn't worn it for ages. And fashion's requirements
Dictate discomfort for men: they must always be dressed in
their finest;
Jackets and boots we must wear, but never night-caps or slippers.

"Look," replied his good wife, "there are some returning
already.
They saw the exiles' procession, which now must almost
be over.
See how dusty their shoes are, and faces aglow with exertion, 40
Every handkerchief out, to wipe away perspiration.
I wouldn't venture so far in this heat to see such
excitement.
Hearing the story suffices. I am contented to listen."

Then to this the father replied with emphatic expression:
"Rarely has weather like this produced such a wonderful harvest.

Und wir bringen die Frucht herein, wie das Heu schon
herein ist,
Trocken; der Himmel ist hell, es ist kein Wölkchen zu sehen,
Und von Morgen wehet der Wind mit lieblicher Kühlung.
Das ist beständiges Wetter! und überreif ist das Korn schon;
Morgen fangen wir an zu schneiden die reichliche Ernte.

Als er so sprach, vermehrten sich immer die Scharen der
Männer
Und der Weiber, die über den Markt sich nach Hause
begaben;
Und so kam auch zurück mit seinen Töchtern gefahren
Rasch, an die andere Seite des Markts, der begüterte
Nachbar,
An sein erneuertes Haus, der erste Kaufmann des Ortes,
Im geöffneten Wagen (er war in Landau verfertigt).
Lebhaft wurden die Gassen; denn wohl war bevölkert das
Städtchen,
Mancher Fabriken befliß man sich da, und manches
Gewerbes.

Und so saß das trauliche Paar, sich, unter dem Torweg,
Über das wandernde Volk mit mancher Bemerkung
ergötzend.
Endlich aber begann die würdige Hausfrau, und sagte:
Seht! dort kommt der Prediger her; es kommt auch der
Nachbar
Apotheker mit ihm: die sollen uns alles erzählen,
Was sie draußen gesehn und was zu schauen nicht froh
macht.

Freundlich kamen heran die beiden, und grüßten
das Ehpaar,
Setzten sich auf die Bänke, die hölzernen, unter dem Torweg,
Staub von den Füßen schüttelnd, und Luft mit dem Tuche
sich fächelnd.

Dry we will gather our fruits, as dry as we gathered
the hay in.
Not the tiniest cloud can be seen all over the sky; and
Easterly breezes bring us delightlful refreshment, with promise
Of the steadiest weather. Already the grain is too ripe, and
In the morning we start to reap our plentiful harvest." 50

As he continued to speak the number of people kept growing,
Crossing the square toward their homes; among them their
wealthiest neighbor.
He was a merchant in town, who owned a fine carriage, in
which he
Rapidly drove toward his house, which had just undergone
renovation.
("Landau" the carriage was called, being named for the town
of its making.)
Riches he had, and prestige, and was widely admired and
respected.
With him his daughters were sitting. The streets became
ever more lively,
For the town had many inhabitants, industries, craftsmen.
There by the entrance in comfort sat the amiable couple,
Watching the crowds pass by and amusing each other 60
with comments.
Finally however the dame of the house made this observation:
"Look, our pastor is coming this way, and with him the druggist,
Our friend. They will be happy to tell us what they have witnessed
Out there; even though seeing it saddened them, still
they will tell us."
Pleasantly both of the men, drawing closer, greeted
the couple;
Seated themselves on benches of wood, which were close by
the gateway,
Shaking the dust from their feet and fanning their faces with
kerchiefs.

Da begann denn zuerst, nach wechselseitigen Grüßen,
Der Apotheker zu sprechen und sagte, beinahe verdrießlich:
So sind die Menschen fürwahr! und einer ist doch wie der andre,
Daß er zu gaffen sich freut, wenn den Nächsten ein Unglück befället!
Läuft doch jeder, die Flamme zu sehn, die verderblich emporschlägt,
Jeder den armen Verbrecher, der peinlich zum Tode geführt wird.
Jeder spaziert nun hinaus, zu schauen der guten Vertriebnen
Elend, und niemand bedenkt, daß ihn das ähnliche Schicksal
Auch, vielleicht zunächst, betreffen kann, oder doch künftig.
Unverzeihlich find ich den Leichtsinn; doch liegt er im Menschen.

Und es sagte darauf der edle verständige Pfarrherr,
Er, die Zierde der Stadt, ein Jüngling näher dem Manne.
Dieser kannte das Leben, und kannte der Hörer Bedürfnis,
War vom hohen Werte der heiligen Schriften durchdrungen,
Die uns der Menschen Geschick enthüllen, und ihre Gesinnung;
Und so kannt er auch wohl die besten weltlichen Schriften.
Dieser sprach: Ich tadle nicht gern, was immer dem Menschen
Für unschädliche Triebe die gute Mutter Natur gab;
Denn was Verstand und Vernunft nicht immer vermögen, vermag oft
Solch ein glücklicher Hang, der unwiderstehlich uns leitet.
Lockte die Neugier nicht den Menschen mit heftigen Reizen,
Sagt! erführ er wohl je, wie schön sich die weltlichen Dinge
Gegeneinander verhalten? Denn erst verlangt er das Neue,
Suchet das Nützliche dann mit unermüdetem Fleiße;
Endlich begehrt er das Gute, das ihn erhebet und wert macht.

Then, after mutual greetings, the first to speak was the druggist.
He was quite annoyed, it would seem, as he said with vexation:
"That's what people are like—and one is as bad as another: 70
Standing with open mouths, and gaping at other's misfortunes.
Everyone hurries to watch when a fire threatens dreadful
disaster;
Everyone runs to behold a criminal dragged to the scaffold.
Everyone now is afoot to observe the distress of these exiles.
Nobody thinks that a similar fate will ever
befall him,
Now or in future. I cannot pardon such folly; but humans
Were in fact born to be stupid." Thus spoke the
garrulous druggist.

And unto this the noble intelligent pastor responded:
(He was the pride of the city: young but mature in his wisdom.
He was acquainted with life and aware of the needs of 80
his people,
Steeped in the lore of the Scriptures, and deeply convinced
of their value,
Since they reveal to mankind its fate and its best dispositions;
Thoroughly trained he was too in the flower of secular learning.)
So he spoke: "I am very reluctant to censure whatever
Nature gave to mankind in the way of innocent instincts;
For what reason and judgment sometimes fail to
accomplish
Often a fortunate chance brings about, if we follow our impulse.
If with its powerful charms curiosity did not entice man,
Tell me, how would he learn the wonderful way in which
Nature
Fits things together? For first he desires what is new to 90
his senses;
Next he seeks what is useful, with tireless and diligent effort;
Lastly he craves after Good, which uplifts him to fulness
of stature.

In der Jugend ist ihm ein froher Gefährte der Leichtsinn,
Der die Gefahr ihm verbirgt, und heilsam geschwinde die Spuren
Tilget des schmerzlichen Übels, sobald es nur irgend vorbeizog.
Freilich ist er zu preisen, der Mann, dem in reiferen Jahren
Sich der gesetzte Verstand aus solchem Frohsinn entwickelt,
Der im Glück wie im Unglück sich eifrig und tätig bestrebet;
Denn das Gute bringt er hervor und ersetzet den Schaden.

Freundlich begann sogleich die ungeduldige Hausfrau:
Saget uns, was ihr gesehn; denn das begehrt ich zu wissen.

Schwerlich, versetzte darauf der Apotheker mit Nachdruck,
Werd ich so bald mich freun nach dem, was ich alles erfahren.
Und wer erzählet es wohl, das mannigfaltigste Elend!
Schon von ferne sahn wir den Staub, noch eh wir die Wiesen
Abwärts kamen; der Zug war schon von Hügel zu Hügel
Unabsehlich dahin, man konnte wenig erkennen.
Als wir nun aber den Weg, der quer durch's Tal geht, erreichten,
War Gedräng und Getümmel noch groß der Wandrer und Wagen.
Leider sahen wir noch genug der Armen vorbeiziehn,
Konnten einzeln erfahren, wie bitter die schmerzliche Flucht sei,
Und wie froh das Gefühl des eilig geretteten Lebens.
Traurig war es zu sehn, die mannigfaltige Habe,
Die ein Haus nur verbirgt, das wohlversehne, und die ein
Guter Wirt umher an die rechten Stellen gesetzt hat,
Immer bereit zum Gebrauche, denn alles ist nötig und nützlich,
Nun zu sehen das alles, auf mancherlei Wagen und Karren
Durcheinander geladen, mit Übereilung geflüchtet.

While he is young his lightness of heart is a joyful companion,
Hiding the perils of life and quickly erasing the traces
Left by the passage of pain, as soon as ever it passes.
He is of course to be praised, whose lightness of heart
is developed
As he grows older, into a settled intelligent judgment;
Who in misfortune and welfare alike is active and eager.
He is productive of good and restores what evil has damaged."

Pleasantly, yet not concealing impatience, the housewife
responded: 100
"Tell us all you have seen, for to hear about this I have waited!"

"Hard will it be to be happy," emphatically answered the
druggist,
"After all I have seen of these wandering, miserable exiles.
Who could ever describe their extensive and varied afflictions?
Far in the distance we noticed the dust, as we came by
the pasture;
Mile after mile the procession extended over the landscape;
Far as the eye could see; yet no details were apparent.
But when we finally came to the road which traverses
the valley,
Great were the crowds and confusion of all the exiles
and wagons.
To our distress we beheld unnumbered people a-marching, 110
Thus we could learn from a few how bitter their sorrowful
flight was,
Yet how joyous the feeling of life thus hastily salvaged.
Sad was that sight; all their possessions scattered about them,
Things that belong in a house, secure in peaceful abundance,
Put by a sensible owner wherever he best can arrange them,
Ready always for use, since all is needed and useful.
What a pity to see so many things in disorder!
Loaded on wagons and barrows, rescued in haste from the
houses;

Über dem Schranke lieget das Sieb und die wollene Decke;
In dem Backtrog das Bett, und das Leintuch über dem
Spiegel.
Ach! und es nimmt die Gefahr, wie wir beim Brande vor
zwanzig
Jahren auch wohl gesehn, dem Menschen alle Besinnung,
Daß er das Unbedeutende faßt, und das Teure zurückläßt.
Also führten auch hier, mit unbesonnener Sorgfalt,
Schlechte Dinge sie fort, die Ochsen und Pferde beschwerend:
Alte Bretter und Fässer, den Gänsestall und den Käfig.
Auch so keuchten die Weiber und Kinder mit Bündeln sich
schleppend,
Unter Körben und Butten voll Sachen keines Gebrauches;
Denn es verläßt der Mensch so ungern das Letzte der Habe.
Und so zog auf dem staubigen Weg der drängende Zug fort,
Ordnungslos und verwirrt. Mit schwächeren Tieren, der eine
Wünschte langsam zu fahren, ein andrer emsig zu eilen.
Da entstand ein Geschrei der gequetschten Weiber und
Kinder,
Und ein Blöken des Viehes, dazwischen der Hunde Gebelfer,
Und ein Wehlaut der Alten und Kranken, die hoch auf dem
schweren
Übergepackten Wagen auf Betten saßen und schwankten.
Aber, aus dem Gleise gedrängt, nach dem Rande des
Hochwegs
Irrte das knarrende Rad; es stürzt' in den Graben das
Fuhrwerk,
Umgeschlagen, und weithin entstürzten im Schwunge die
Menschen,
Mit entsetzlichem Schrein, in das Feld hin, aber doch
glücklich.
Später stürzten die Kasten, und fielen näher dem Wagen.
Wahrlich, wer im Fallen sie sah, der erwartete nun sie
Unter der Last der Kisten und Schränke zerschmettert zu
schauen.
Und so lag zerbrochen der Wagen, und hülflos die Menschen;

Woolen blankets share with a sieve the top of the bureau;
Quilts lie stuffed in a trough, and a tablecloth covers the mirror. 120
Danger, alas, robs men of their senses, as we ourselves realized
Twenty years ago, at the time of the fire in our city,
So that they rescue the useless and leave what is precious behind them.
These unfortunates also are carrying, foolishly careful,
All sorts of useless equipment, and overloading their oxen;
Barrels and old boards, goosepens, cages, and similar rubbish.
So then the women and children were struggling along with their bundles
Under the weight of the baskets and boxes of no use whatever,
For thus reluctant are people to part with the last of their chattels.
Thus on the dust-covered road the disorderly marchers proceeded, 130
Pushing, confused, and distracted. One with slow-footed horses
Drove at a leisurely pace, while others insisted on speeding;
Then there arose a cry of distress from women and children;
Animals bleated in anguish, and every dog started barking;
Exclamations of pain were heard from the sick and the aged,
Perching precarious there on the very top of the wagon.
Then the wheel, pushed out of the rut by the pressure of traffic,
Suddenly squeaked, and slipped toward the edge of the roadway; the wagon
Tumbled into the ditch, and the passengers speedily scattered,
Terribly screaming, over the field, yet still got off lightly. 140
After a moment the boxes landed close to the wagon.
Truthfully, we were afraid as we watched the disaster that someone
Under the weight of the boxes and chests would be shattered and broken.
There lay the vehicle, hopelessly ruined, and helpless its owners:

Denn die übrigen gingen und zogen eilig vorüber,
Nur sich selber bedenkend und hingerissen vom Strome.
Und wir eilten hinzu, und fanden die Kranken und Alten,
Die zu Haus und im Bett schon kaum ihr dauerndes Leiden
Trügen, hier auf dem Boden, beschädigt, ächzen und jammern,
Von der Sonne verbrannt und erstickt vom wogenden Staube.

Und es sagte darauf, gerührt, der menschliche Hauswirt:
Möge doch Hermann sie treffen und sie erquicken und kleiden.
Ungern würd ich sie sehn; mich schmerzt der Anblick des Jammers.
Schon von dem ersten Bericht so großer Leiden gerühret,
Schickten wir eilend ein Scherflein von unserm Überfluß, daß nur
Einige würden gestärkt, und schienen uns selber beruhigt.
Aber laßt uns nicht mehr die traurigen Bilder erneuern;
Denn es beschleichet die Furcht gar bald die Herzen der Menschen,
Und die Sorge, die mehr als selbst mir das Übel verhaßt ist.
Tretet herein in den hinteren Raum, das kühlere Sälchen.
Nie scheint Sonne dahin, nie dringet wärmere Luft dort
Durch die stärkeren Mauern; und Mütterchen bringt uns ein Gläschen
Dreiundachtziger her, damit wir die Grillen vertreiben.
Hier ist nicht freundlich zu trinken; die Fliegen umsummen die Gläser.
Und sie gingen dahin und freuten sich alle der Kühlung.

Sorgsam brachte die Mutter des klaren herrlichen Weines,
In geschliffener Flasche auf blankem zinnernem Runde,
Mit den grünlichen Römern, den echten Bechern des Rheinweins.—
Und so sitzend umgaben die drei den glänzend gebohnten,
Runden, braunen Tisch, er stand auf mächtigen Füßen.

All the rest of the exiles marched unfeelingly past them,
Thinking only of self and carried along by the others.
We came hurrying up and found the sick and the aged,
Who in the comfort of home and in bed would be
scarcely surviving,
Here on the ground in their wretchedness groaning and
pleading for mercy,
Burned by the heat of the sun and smothered by dust from 150
the highway."

Thereunto with emotion the amiable innkeeper answered:
"Hermann, I hope, will soon meet them and bring them
refreshment and clothing.
I would not like to see them, for I find misery painful.
Moved by the very first rumor of these poor exiles' afflictions
We have already sent them a mite from our superabundance,
So that some may be strengthened; and thus our hearts
are untroubled.
But let us now no longer renew these sorrowful pictures!
For our hearts can be easily seized by the spectres of terror
And anxiety, which for myself I detest even more than
Evil . . . Just come with me to the taproom where it is cooler. 160
There the sun never shines, and the room is never too stuffy;
Since the walls are so thick. Let Mother bring us a bottle:
'Eighty-three would be best to chase away our depression.
Here we cannot drink in peace for the buzzing flies in the glasses."
So they went in and rejoiced in the coolness together.

Carefully then the good housewife presently brought them
the glasses,
Filled from a well-polished bottle on a shining salver of pewter.
Rhine wine she brought, and the glasses were greenish. Rummers
they called them.
So then they sat, surrounding the table, which sparkled with polish;
Round was the table and brown, supported by legs of great 170
thickness.

Heiter klangen sogleich die Gläser des Wirtes und Pfarrers;
Doch unbeweglich hielt der dritte denkend das seine,
Und es fordert' ihn auf der Wirt mit freundlichen Worten:

Frisch, Herr Nachbar, getrunken! denn noch bewahrte vor Unglück
Gott uns gnädig, und wird auch künftig uns also bewahren.
Denn wer erkennet es nicht, daß seit dem schrecklichen Brande
Da er so hart uns gestraft, er uns nun beständig erfreut hat,
Und beständig beschützt, so wie der Mensch sich des Auges
Köstlichen Apfel bewahrt, der vor allen Gliedern ihm lieb ist.
Sollt er fernerhin nicht uns schützen und Hülfe bereiten?
Denn man sieht es erst recht, wie viel er vermag, in Gefahren;
Sollt er die blühende Stadt, die er erst durch fleißige Bürger
Neu aus der Asche gebaut und dann sie reichlich gesegnet,
Jetzo wieder zerstören und alle Bemühung vernichten?

Heiter sagte darauf der treffliche Pfarrer, und milde:
Haltet am Glauben fest, und fest an dieser Gesinnung;
Denn sie macht im Glücke verständig und sicher, im Unglück
Reicht sie den schönsten Trost und belebt die herrlichste Hoffnung.

Da versetzte der Wirt, mit männlichen klugen Gedanken:
Wie begrüßt ich so oft mit Staunen die Fluten des Rheinstroms,
Wenn ich, reisend nach meinem Geschäft, ihm wieder mich nahte!
Immer schien er mir groß, und erhob mir Sinn und Gemüte;
Aber ich konnte nicht denken, daß bald sein liebliches Ufer
Sollte werden ein Wall, um abzuwehren den Franken,

Pastor and host lost no time in cheerfully clinking their glasses;
But the druggist pensively held his own glass suspended.
So then the host exhorted his guest with kind admonition:
"Come, good neighbor, drink up! For God has preserved us from evil
So far, and in future will likewise graciously save us.
For we can easily see, since the terrible fire, when He punished
Us severely, that now He has constantly given us cause for
Gladness, and always protected our city, as men give protection,
Carefully shielding, to eyesight, most precious of all their possessions.
God will continue to help us and give us His gracious protection. 180
For when danger approaches the Father shows how He loves us:
Would He destroy this flourishing city, rebuilt only lately,
With the assistance of diligent citizens, fresh from the fire, and
Which He has blessed with abundance, thus making futile our labor?"

Cheerfully then, without harshness, the excellent pastor responded:
"Keep the faith and be loyal to this your unwavering position!
For in good fortune it gives life meaning and safety; but when your
Fortune is evil it comforts, and quickens fair hopes amid suff'ring."
Thereto the innkeeper said, with intelligent, manly reflection:
"How I welcomed, with joyous surprise, the floods of the Rhine stream, 190
When from my travels I came once again to the shores of our river!
Always it seemed to me grand, and uplifted my mind and my spirits;
Yet I never could dream that so soon its beautiful borders
Would be used as a wall to defend ourselves from the Frenchmen,

Und sein verbreitetes Bett ein allverhindernder Graben.
Seht, so schützt die Natur, so schützen die wackeren Deutschen
Und so schützt uns der Herr; wer wollte töricht verzagen?
Müde schon sind die Streiter, und alles deutet auf Frieden.
Möge doch auch, wenn das Fest, das lang erwünschte, gefeiert
Wird, in unserer Kirche, die Glocke dann tönt zu der Orgel,
Und die Trompete schmettert, das hohe Te Deum begleitend,
Möge mein Hermann doch auch an diesem Tage, Herr Pfarrer,
Mit der Braut, entschlossen, vor euch, am Altare, sich stellen,
Und das glückliche Fest, in allen den Landen begangen,
Auch mir künftig erscheinen, der häuslichen Freuden ein Jahrstag!
Aber ungern seh ich den Jüngling, der immer so tätig
Mir in dem Hause sich regt, nach außen langsam und schüchtern.
Wenig findet er Lust sich unter Leuten zu zeigen;
Ja, er vermeidet sogar der jungen Mädchen Gesellschaft,
Und den fröhlichen Tanz, den alle Jugend begehret.

Also sprach er und horchte. Man hörte der stampfenden Pferde
Fernes Getöse sich nahn, man hörte den rollenden Wagen,
Der mit gewaltiger Eile nun donnert' unter den Torweg.

And its broadspreading bed would become an impassable barrier.
See, we are guarded by Nature, by undefeatable Germans,
And the Lord Himself is our strength: so how can we falter?
Weary of war are the soldiers, and all the signs point to concord.
When we celebrate peace, when the long expectation is over,
And the people are gathered in church to the peals of the organ, 200
And the reverberant bells, while the trumpet sounds the
Te Deum
Then, on that day, my dear pastor, may Hermann with
firm resolution
Step with his bride to the altar, and you will join them together.
Then that glorious holiday, everywhere bringing men gladness,
I will celebrate yearly, in memory of family rejoicing.
I am not pleased that my son is so timid in social relations.
Though he is active and helpful at home he rarely takes
pleasure
In intermingling with other young people, especially avoiding
Every contact with girls, and even the pleasures of dancing,
Which as you know are the joy and delight of the 210
young generation."

Thus he spoke, then suddenly listened. The hooves of the horses,
Heard in the distance, came closer, the noisy wheels of
the carriage,
Rolled with wondrous rapidity, thundering, under the gateway.

II

TERPSICHORE

Hermann

Als nun der wohlgebildete Sohn ins Zimmer hereintrat,
Schaute der Prediger ihm mit scharfen Blicken entgegen,
Und betrachtete seine Gestalt und sein ganzes Benehmen,
Mit dem Auge des Forschers, der leicht die Mienen enträtselt;
Lächelte dann, und sprach zu ihm mit traulichen Worten:
Kommt ihr doch als ein veränderter Mensch! Ich habe noch
niemals
Euch so munter gesehn und eure Blicke so lebhaft.
Fröhlich kommt ihr und heiter; man sieht, ihr habet die
Gaben
Unter die Armen verteilt und ihren Segen empfangen.

Ruhig erwiderte drauf der Sohn, mit ernstlichen Worten:
Ob ich löblich gehandelt? ich weiß es nicht; aber mein
Herz hat
Mich geheißen zu tun, so wie ich genau nun erzähle.
Mutter, ihr kramtet so lange, die alten Stücke zu suchen
Und zu wählen; nur spät war erst das Bündel zusammen,
Auch der Wein und das Bier ward langsam, sorglich
gepacket.
Als ich nun endlich vors Tor und auf die Straße hinauskam,
Strömte zurück die Menge der Bürger mit Weibern und
Kindern,
Mir entgegen; denn fern war schon der Zug der Vertriebnen.
Schneller hielt ich mich dran, und fuhr behende dem
Dorf zu,

II

TERPSICHORE

Hermann

When now the handsome young fellow stepped briskly in
through the doorway,
Quickly, with shrewdest of glances, the pastor examined
his features,
Closely observed his deportment and studied his mien and
his bearing,
(Just as a scientist looks, who reads the meanings of faces)
Smiled then and spoke to the youth, with affectionate greeting,
as follows:
"You are a different person! I never have seen you so lively;
Never such fire in your eyes, such gay expression and gladness.
Clearly the gifts have been given, and you have been richly
rewarded,
Blessed from the heart and abundantly thanked by those who
received them."

Calmly the son replied, and spoke in a serious manner: 10
"Did I do what was right? I know not; however, I followed
Every command of my heart, and now I will tell you the story.
Mother, it took you so long to gather the clothing together,
Choosing the oldest you had, that the bundle was late for
my taking;
Wine and beer were carefully packed so that none might
be wasted.
When then I finally came to the gate and out on the highway,
Crowds of our townsfolk were blocking the road with their wives
and their children,
On their way back, for by now the exiles were far in the distance.
So I quickened the pace and rapidly drove toward the village,

Wo sie, wie ich gehört, heut übernachten und rasten.
Als ich nun meines Weges die neue Straße hinanfuhr,
Fiel mir ein Wagen ins Auge, von tüchtigen Bäumen gefüget,
Von zwei Ochsen gezogen, den größten und stärksten des Auslands,
Nebenher aber ging, mit starken Schritten, ein Mädchen.
Lenkte mit langem Stabe die beiden gewaltigen Tiere,
Trieb sie an und hielt sie zurück, sie leitete klüglich.

Als mich das Mädchen erblickte, so trat sie den Pferden gelassen
Näher und sagte zu mir: Nicht immer war es mit uns so
Jammervoll, als ihr uns heut auf diesen Wegen erblicket.
Noch nicht bin ich gewohnt, vom Fremden die Gabe zu heischen,
Die er oft ungern gibt, um los zu werden den Armen;
Aber mich dränget die Not zu reden. Hier auf dem Strohe
Liegt die erst entbundene Frau des reichen Besitzers,
Die ich mit Stieren und Wagen noch kaum, die Schwangre, gerettet.

Spät nur kommen wir nach, und kaum das Leben erhielt sie.
Nun liegt, neugeboren, das Kind ihr nackend im Arme,
Und mit wenigem nur vermögen die unsern zu helfen,
Wenn wir im nächsten Dorf, wo wir heute zu rasten gedenken,
Auch sie finden, wiewohl ich fürchte, sie sind schon vorüber.
Wär euch irgend von Leinwand nur was Entbehrliches, wenn ihr
Hier aus der Nachbarschaft seid, so spendet's gütig den Armen.

Where, as I heard, they are planning to stay for the night 20
and recover.
Whilst I was driving along on my way toward the newly
constructed
Road, a wagon caught my attention, built from enormous
Beams, which was drawn by a pair of the largest and strongest
of oxen,
Led by a girl who was walking sturdily, next to the wagon,
Holding a staff to control the lumbering, powerful oxen.
How well she drove, urging them on, or holding them quiet!
When the young woman beheld me she stepped right up to
the horses,
Close by their heads, and addressed me: 'Our state, as you see
it this moment,
Here on this wagon, is much more wretched than ever it has
been;
Still I am quite unaccustomed to begging for kindness 30
from strangers,
Which is bestowed with reluctance and just to get rid of
the beggar.
Need now compels me, however, to speak, for here on this litter
Lies a woman who used to be rich, who has just been delivered.
Barely I managed to save her, though pregnant, by means
of this oxcart.
We have lagged far behind; she has barely escaped with survival.
Now her infant just born, lies naked there in her arms, and
Only a little can our people help them, if ever we find them,
There in the village beyond here, where we intend to
seek shelter.
Though I most seriously fear they have already reached it and
passed it.
If you have linen to spare, if you come from the neighborhood 40
here, then
Please let them have some, for they are in desperate need of
your kindness.'

Also sprach sie, und matt erhob sich vom Strohe die bleiche
Wöchnerin, schaute nach mir; ich aber sagte dagegen:
Guten Menschen, fürwahr, spricht oft ein himmlischer
Geist zu,
Daß sie fühlen die Not, die dem armen Bruder bevorsteht;
Denn so gab mir die Mutter, im Vorgefühle von eurem
Jammer, ein Bündel, sogleich es der nackten Notdurft zu
reichen.
Und ich löste die Knoten der Schnur, und gab ihr den
Schlafrock
Unsers Vaters dahin, und gab ihr Hemden und Leintuch.
Und sie dankte mit Freuden, und rief: Der Glückliche
glaubt nicht,
Daß noch Wunder geschehn; denn nur im Elend erkennt
man
Gottes Hand und Finger, der gute Menschen zum Guten
Leitet. Was er durch euch an uns tut, tu er euch selber.

Und ich sah die Wöchnerin froh die verschiedene Leinwand,
Aber besonders den weichen Flanell des Schlafrocks
befühlen.
Eilen wir, sagte zu ihr die Jungfrau, dem Dorf zu, in
welchem
Unsre Gemeine schon rastet und diese Nacht durch sich
aufhält;
Dort besorg ich sogleich das Kinderzeug, alles und jedes.
Und sie grüßte mich noch, und sprach den herzlichsten
Dank aus,
Trieb die Ochsen; da ging der Wagen. Ich aber verweilte,
Hielt die Pferde noch an; denn Zwiespalt war mir im Herzen,
Ob ich mit eilenden Rossen das Dorf erreichte, die Speisen
Unter das übrige Volk zu spenden, oder sogleich hier
Alles dem Mädchen gäbe, damit sie es weislich verteilte.
Und ich entschied mich gleich in meinem Herzen,
und fuhr ihr
Sachte nach, und erreichte sie bald, und sagte behende:

Thus spoke the maiden, and weakly there rose from the
straw the exhausted
Form of the mother, looking at me, but I told her in answer:
'Truly a heavenly spirit frequently motivates deeds of
Kindness from those who are good, to aid the distressed
and afflicted;
Thus the presentiment of my good mother, of all your
misfortune,
Caused me to bring you, for instant relief of the needy,
this package.'
And I untied the knot of the cord and I gave her the housecoat
Which had belonged to my father, and gave her the shirts and
the linen.
Then she thanked me with joy and exclaimed: 'The man who
is happy 50
Does not believe in a miracle, since in misfortune alone we
Recognize God's operation in leading the good to do good. Now
As He has done unto us through you, may He ever
requite you!'
Then I saw how the woman was feeling the various linens
Joyfully, but above all the flannel soft of the housecoat.
'Let us hurry,' the maiden said to her then, 'to the village
Where our companions will stay for the night and already
are resting;
There I will work right away on the clothes for the baby, who
needs them.'
Then she cordially waved and thanked me again for our gifts and
Started her oxen and wagon, while I, in some hesitation, 60
Lingered behind with my horses, for still my mind was uncertain
Whether to speed to the village and give all the food to
the others
Or to give everything here to the girl to distribute discreetly.
Then in my heart I decided and followed quietly after.
Soon I caught up with the maiden and spoke, without hesitation:

Gutes Mädchen, mir hat die Mutter nicht Leinwand alleine
Auf den Wagen gegeben, damit ich den Nackten bekleide,
Sondern sie fügte dazu noch Speis und manches Getränke,
Und es ist mir genug davon im Kasten des Wagens.
Nun bin ich aber geneigt, auch diese Gaben in deine
Hand zu legen, und so erfüll ich am besten den Auftrag;
Du verteilst sie mit Sinn, ich müßte dem Zufall gehorchen.
Drauf versetzte das Mädchen: Mit aller Treue verwend ich
Eure Gaben; der Dürftige soll sich derselben erfreuen.
Also sprach sie. Ich öffnete schnell die Kasten des Wagens,
Brachte die Schinken hervor, die schweren, brachte die Brote,
Flaschen Weines und Biers, und reicht ihr alles und jedes.
Gerne hätt ich noch mehr ihr gegeben; doch leer war der Kasten.
Alles packte sie drauf zu der Wöchnerin Füßen, und zog so
Weiter; ich eilte zurück mit meinen Pferden der Stadt zu.

Als nun Hermann geendet, da nahm der gesprächige Nachbar
Gleich das Wort, und rief: O glücklich, wer in den Tagen
Dieser Flucht und Verwirrung in seinem Haus nur allein lebt,
Wem nicht Frau und Kinder zur Seite bange sich schmiegen!
Glücklich fühl ich mich jetzt; ich möcht um vieles nicht heute
Vater heißen und nicht für Frau und Kinder besorgt sein.
Öfters dacht ich mir auch schon die Flucht, und habe die besten
Sachen zusammengepackt, das alte Geld und die Ketten
Meiner seligen Mutter, das alles noch heilig verwahrt liegt.
Freilich bliebe noch vieles zurück, das so leicht nicht geschafft wird.

'Excellent maiden, my mother has laden my carriage not only
With the linen for clothing the naked, but also she added
Food to nourish the body, and various drinks for refreshment.
There in the box of the wagon I have them all ready, in plenty. 70
I am however inclined at this moment to put you in charge of
Everything; thus I fulfill my commission most wisely and
well, for
You will distribute it fairly, while I would be acting at random.'
Thereupon answered the maiden: 'Faithfully I will distribute
Your gifts; those who are needy will get them, and hearts will
be gladdened.'
As she was speaking I quickly opened the box of the wagon,
Brought out the hams and the bread in abundance, and bottles
of wine and
Beer, and gave her it all to take to her needy companions.
Glad would I be to have given her more, but the boxes
were empty.
Then, having stowed it away at the new mother's feet, 80
she departed,
But with my swift-footed horses I rapidly drove toward the city."

After Hermann had finished the talkative neighbor began to
Speak and exclaimed: "O happy is he who in time of confusion
And of displacement can live by himself alone in his dwelling,
Free from the clinging involvement of timorous women
and children.
Lucky I feel myself now: for today I am glad to be childless,
Free from concern about children and wife in this time of
our peril.
Often I thought I might flee with the rest, and I packed my
belongings,
All of my favorite things: old coins and chains which belonged to
Mother, may she rest in peace, which I kept with most 90
tender devotion.
Naturally much would be left which I could not so easily carry;

Selbst die Kräuter und Wurzeln, mit vielem Fleiße gesammelt,
Mißt ich ungern, wenn auch der Wert der Ware nicht
groß ist.
Bleibt der Provisor zurück, so geh ich getröstet von Hause.
Hab ich die Barschaft gerettet und meinen Körper,
so hab ich
Alles gerettet; der einzelne Mann entfliehet am leichtsten.

Nachbar, versetzte darauf der junge Hermann, mit
Nachdruck:
Keinesweges denk ich wie ihr und tadle die Rede.
Ist wohl der ein würdiger Mann, der, im Glück und im
Unglück,
Sich nur allein bedenkt, und Leiden und Freuden zu teilen
Nicht verstehet, und nicht dazu von Herzen bewegt wird?
Lieber möcht ich, als je, mich heute zur Heirat entschließen;
Denn manch gutes Mädchen bedarf des schützenden
Mannes,
Und der Mann des erheiternden Weibs, wenn ihm Unglück
bevorsteht.
Lächelnd sagte darauf der Vater: So hör ich dich gerne!
Solch ein vernünftiges Wort hast du mir selten gesprochen.

Aber es fiel sogleich die gute Mutter behend ein:
Sohn, fürwahr! du hast recht; wir Eltern gaben das Beispiel.
Denn wir haben uns nicht an fröhlichen Tagen erwählet,
Und uns knüpfte vielmehr die traurigste Stunde zusammen.
Montag morgens—ich weiß es genau; denn Tages
vorher war
Jener schreckliche Brand, der unser Städtchen verzehrte—
Zwanzig Jahre sind's nun; es war ein Sonntag wie heute,
Heiß und trocken die Zeit, und wenig Wasser im Orte.
Alle Leute waren, spazierend in festlichen Kleidern,
Auf den Dörfern verteilt und in den Schenken und Mühlen.
Und am Ende der Stadt begann das Feuer. Der Brand lief
Eilig die Straßen hindurch, erzeugend sich selber den
Zugwind.

Even the herbs and the roots which I gathered with care and with patience,
I would not like to forsake, though their value is not very striking.
If my assistant would stay, I could leave without any worry.
If I have rescued my cash and my person, have I not rescued
Everything? All by oneself one escapes in the easiest fashion."

Hermann responded to this most emphatically, saying, "Good neighbor,
Not in the least do I share your opinion. I censure you for it.
Is there a man worth the name, who in fortunate time or in evil
Thinks of himself all alone, unable to share in the joys and 100
Sorrows of others, unmoved in his heart, and unwilling to share them?
Rather, today more than ever before I would like to get married,
For there is many a girl who requires a husband's protection,
And a man has a need of a comforting wife in misfortune."
Smiling his father responded: "These are remarks that I like, and
Seldom that I can remember have you ever spoken so wisely."

But the excellent mother at once interrupted her husband:
"Son, indeed you are right; it was we who set the example.
Not on a day of rejoicing did we announce our betrothal.
Rather the saddest of moments witnessed our joining together. 110
Monday it was, in the morning, I clearly remember it; only
One day after the terrible fire had wasted our city.
Twenty years have gone by: it was Sunday, just like today, and
Hot was the weather, and dry, and the water was almost exhausted.
Everyone, clothed in his best, was out for a walk in the country,
Some in the neighboring villages, others in mills and in taverns.
Down at the end of the city the fire began, and it raced with
Speed through the streets, creating a current of air for itself, and

Und es brannten die Scheunen der reichgesammelten Ernte,
Und es brannten die Straßen bis zu dem Markt, und das Haus war
Meines Vaters hierneben verzehrt, und dieses zugleich mit.
Wenig flüchteten wir. Ich saß, die traurige Nacht durch,
Vor der Stadt auf dem Anger, die Kasten und Betten bewahrend;
Doch zuletzt befiel mich der Schlaf, und als nun des Morgens
Mich die Kühlung erweckte, die vor der Sonne herabfällt,
Sah ich den Rauch und die Glut und die hohlen Mauern und Essen.
Da war beklemmt mein Herz; allein die Sonne ging wieder
Herrlicher auf als je, und flößte mir Mut in die Seele.
Da erhob ich mich eilend. Es trieb mich, die Stätte zu sehen,
Wo die Wohnung gestanden, und ob sich die Hühner gerettet,
Die ich besonders geliebt; denn kindisch war mein Gemüt noch.
Als ich nun über die Trümmer des Hauses und Hofes daher stieg,
Die noch rauchten, und so die Wohnung wüst und zerstört sah,
Kamst du zur andern Seite herauf, und durchsuchtest die Stätte.
Dir war ein Pferd in dem Stalle verschüttet; die glimmenden Balken
Lagen darüber und Schutt, und nichts zu sehn war vom Tiere.
Also standen wir gegeneinander, bedenklich und traurig:
Denn die Wand war gefallen, die unsere Höfe geschieden.
Und du faßtest darauf mich bei der Hand an, und sagtest:
Lieschen, wie kommst du hieher? Geh weg! du verbrennest die Sohlen;

Soon the abundance of grain in the barns was aflame, and
aflame were
All of the houses lining the streets on the way to the market; 120
Now the house of my father next door to us here was
consumed, and
Very soon this one as well, so that not very much could
be rescued.
All through the sorrowful night I sat in the meadow, protecting
All our bedgear and boxes, until I succumbed to fatigue, and
When in the morning the coolness that comes before sunrise
awoke me,
Then I could see the smoke and the glow of the walls and
the chimneys,
Hollowed by fire, and my heart sank within me. The sun
nonetheless was
Rising again, more splendid than ever, infusing my soul with
Courage. Then quickly I rose, for I wanted to see where
the house had
Stood, and whether the chickens, so dear to my heart, had 130
been rescued.
(For I was still like a child in my feelings.) And when I had
climbed through
All the ruins of household and farm, still fuming and glowing,
There I could see the desolate dwelling, destroyed by the
flames; but
You then arrived from the other direction to search through
the ruins.
You had a horse that was buried under the barn, and the glowing
Beams lay above it, and rubble, and nothing was to be seen. So
There then we stood, reflective and sorrowful, close to each other,
For the wall which divided our houses was standing no longer.
Then you took hold of my hand and said to me: "Lisa!
Whatever
Can you be doing here? You must leave here at once, for your 140
feet are

Denn der Schutt ist heiß, er sengt mir die stärkeren Stiefeln.
Und du hobest mich auf, und trugst mich herüber, durch deinen
Hof weg. Da stand noch das Tor des Hauses mit seinem Gewölbe,
Wie es jetzt steht; es war allein von allem geblieben.
Und du setztest mich nieder und küßtest mich und ich verwehrt es.
Aber du sagtest darauf mit freundlich bedeutenden Worten:
Siehe, das Haus liegt nieder. Bleib hier, und hilf mir es bauen,
Und ich helfe dagegen auch deinem Vater an seinem.
Doch ich verstand dich nicht, bis du zum Vater die Mutter
Schicktest und schnell das Gelübd der fröhlichen Ehe vollbracht war.
Noch erinnr' ich mich heute des halbverbrannten Gebälkes
Freudig, und sehe die Sonne noch immer so herrlich heraufgehn;
Denn mir gab der Tag den Gemahl, es haben die ersten
Zeiten der wilden Zerstörung den Sohn mir der Jugend gegeben.
Darum lob ich dich, Hermann, daß du mit reinem Vertrauen
Auch ein Mädchen dir denkst in diesen traurigen Zeiten,
Und es wagtest zu frein im Krieg und über den Trümmern.

Da versetzte sogleich der Vater lebhaft und sagte:
Die Gesinnung ist löblich, und wahr ist auch die Geschichte,
Mütterchen, die du erzählst; denn so ist alles begegnet.
Aber besser ist besser. Nicht einen jeden betrifft es
Anzufangen von vorn sein ganzes Leben und Wesen;
Nicht soll jeder sich quälen, wie wir und andere taten,
O, wie glücklich ist der, dem Vater und Mutter das Haus schon
Wohlbestellt übergeben, und der mit Gedeihen es ausziert!
Aller Anfang ist schwer, am schwersten der Anfang der Wirtschaft.

Apt to be scorched, since the ashes are hot and are burning
the soles of
Even my boots." Then you lifted me up and carried me over
Here, through your yard, where the gate of the house was
intact with its archway,
Just as you see it today; it alone had escaped the disaster.
There you lifted me down and kissed me, though I tried to
stop you.
But you said to me then in your warmest, most meaningful
manner,
'Look, the house is destroyed. Stay here and help me rebuild it;
I will contribute my share to your father in rebuilding *his* house.'
But I did not understand you until you had sent to my father
Through your mother a promise, and quickly our marriage
was readied. 150
Even today I clearly remember the half-consumed timbers,
And how joyful I was when the sun rose as splendid as ever,
For that day was to give me my husband: the earliest days of
Our disaster were destined to give me the son of my youth. So
Therefore I praise you, my Hermann, because in the season of
trouble
You are thinking with confidence also of marriage, and even
Daring to seek for a wife in spite of the war and its ruins."

Then the father responded, declaring with promptness and vigor:
"Your way of thinking is worthy of praise, and true is the story,
Mother, which you have told; that is just the way it all happened. 160
But what is better is better. Not every person is able,
Starting all over again, to rebuild his whole life and his fortune.
Nor should everyone worry as we did, along with the others.
O, how happy is he to whom parents can pass on their house, in
Finest condition: the son can embellish the place as he prospers.
Every beginning works hardship, but worst is the start of
a household.

Mancherlei Dinge bedarf der Mensch, und alles wird täglich
Teurer; da seh er sich vor, des Geldes mehr zu erwerben.
Und so hoff ich von dir, mein Hermann, daß du mir
nächstens
In das Haus die Braut mit schöner Mitgift hereinführst;
Denn ein wackerer Mann verdient ein begütertes Mädchen,
Und es behaget so wohl, wenn mit dem gewünscheten
Weibchen,
Auch in Körben und Kasten die nützliche Gabe herein-
kommt.
Nicht umsonst bereitet durch manche Jahre die Mutter
Viele Leinwand der Tochter, von feinem und starkem
Gewebe;
Nicht umsonst verehren die Paten ihr Silbergeräte,
Und der Vater sondert im Pulte das seltene Goldstück:
Denn sie soll dereinst mit ihren Gütern und Gaben
Jenen Jüngling erfreun, der sie vor allen erwählt hat.
Ja, ich weiß, wie behaglich ein Weibchen im Hause sich
findet,
Das ihr eignes Gerät in Küch und Zimmern erkennet,
Und das Bette sich selbst und den Tisch sich selber
gedeckt hat.
Nur wohl ausgestattet möcht ich im Hause die Braut sehn;
Denn die Arme wird doch nur zuletzt vom Manne verachtet,
Und er hält sie als Magd, die als Magd mit dem Bündel
hereinkam.
Ungerecht bleiben die Männer, und die Zeiten der Liebe
vergehen.
Ja, mein Hermann, du würdest mein Alter höchlich erfreuen,
Wenn du mir bald ins Haus ein Schwiegertöchterchen
brächtest
Aus der Nachbarschaft her, aus jenem Hause, dem grünen.
Reich ist der Mann fürwahr: sein Handel und seine
Fabriken
Machen ihn täglich reicher: denn wo gewinnt nicht der
Kaufmann?

Men are in need of so much and the cost keeps ever increasing,
So they must have an eye for the chance of earning more money.
That, my Hermann, is why I must hope you will bring us a daughter
Who has a plentiful dowry; the sooner the better, I tell you. 170
For a competent fellow deserves a propertied maiden,
And it is truly delightful to take, with the helpmeet you wished for,
Also, in baskets and boxes, some practical gifts for the marriage.
Not for nothing has mother been saving for years all her linen,
Woven with beauty and strength, for her daughter to bring into marriage,
Not in vain have the godparents given her silver utensils;
And, when he gets a rare goldpiece, her father will keep it in safety,
For, in the future, her gifts and possessions will gladden the youth who
Chose her alone from the girls of the village to wed and to cherish.
Yes, I know how easy it is for a wife to adjust to 180
Wedlock, when, in the kitchen and bedrooms she sees her utensils,
And when the linen for bed and for table is part of her dowry.
Let a bride be equipped in her home with every convenience,
For a girl without fortune will merit contempt from her husband.
And he will treat as a servant a girl who arrived with a bundle.
Men are prone to injustice, and love is easily forgotten.
Yes, my dear son, you would greatly oblige me, as old age advances,
If you would bring to the house very soon, as your bride, a delightful
Girl from the neighborhood here, from the house over yonder, the green one.
Rich indeed is its owner—his business and factories daily 190
Make him yet richer; for merchants are practically always successful.

Nur drei Töchter sind da; sie teilen allein das Vermögen.
Schon ist die ältste bestimmt, ich weiß es; aber die zweite,
Wie die dritte sind noch, und vielleicht nicht lange, zu haben.
Wär ich an deiner Statt, ich hätte bis jetzt nicht gezaudert,
Eins mir der Mädchen geholt, so wie ich das Mütterchen
forttrug.

Da versetzte der Sohn bescheiden dem dringenden Vater:
Wirklich, mein Wille war auch, wie eurer, eine der Töchter
Unsers Nachbars zu wählen. Wir sind zusammen erzogen,
Spielten neben dem Brunnen am Markt in früheren Zeiten,
Und ich habe sie oft vor der Knaben Wildheit beschützet.
Doch das ist lange schon her; es bleiben die wachsenden
Mädchen
Endlich billig zu Haus, und fliehn die wilderen Spiele.
Wohlgezogen sind sie gewiß! Ich ging auch zu Zeiten
Noch aus alter Bekanntschaft, so wie ihr es wünschtet,
hinüber;
Aber ich konnte mich nie in ihrem Umgang erfreuen.
Denn sie tadelten stets an mir, das mußt ich ertragen:
Gar zu lang war mein Rock, zu grob das Tuch, und die
Farbe
Gar zu gemein, und die Haare nicht recht gestutzt und
gekräuselt.
Endlich hatt ich im Sinne, mich auch zu putzen, wie jene
Handelsbübchen, die stets am Sonntag drüben sich zeigen,
Und um die, halbseiden, im Sommer das Läppchen
herumhängt.
Aber noch früh genug merkt ich, sie hatten mich immer zum
besten;
Und das war mir empfindlich, mein Stolz war beleidigt;
doch mehr noch
Kränkte mich's tief, daß so sie den guten Willen verkannten,
Den ich gegen sie hegte, besonders Minchen die jüngste.

Only three daughters he has to inherit the whole of his fortune.
Now I know that the eldest is promised, but the middle and
youngest
Still are available, even though, probably, not for much longer.
If I were you I would not have shown reluctance to ask for
One of the girls, in the way I proposed long ago to your mother."

Then, to his father's insistence, Hermann respectfully answered:
"Truly I wanted, as you do, to marry one of our neighbor's
Daughters; indeed, we were raised with each other, instructed
together,
Played by the mountain that flows in the square in the years
of our childhood; 200
Often I have protected the girls from the other boys' roughness.
But that is long, long ago; and the girls as they grow
must remain at
Home, as they should, and refuse to join in the boisterous pastimes.
Well-bred surely they are! At times I went over to see them,
Just for the sake of the old days, or just to comply with
your wishes,
But their company never could give me real satisfaction.
For they were always reproving my manners, and I had to bear it;
Much too long was my coat, or too coarse was the cloth, and
the color
Quite undistinguished; my hair was improperly cut and not curly.
After a while I decided to dress like the clerks and the salesmen 210
Who of a Sunday appear over there with constant devotion.
Often in summer you see them with half-silken rags draped
around them.
Soon I could see that they always would mock me, and this
I regretted,
For my pride was offended, and, even more, I was wounded
Deeply, because the good will that I had, especially for Mina,
Who was the youngest, went disregarded. The last time I
went there,

Denn so war ich zuletzt an Ostern hinübergegangen,
Hatte den neuen Rock, der jetzt nur oben im Schrank hängt,
Angezogen und war frisiert wie die übrigen Bursche.
Als ich eintrat, kicherten sie; doch zog ich's auf mich nicht.
Minchen saß am Klavier; es war der Vater zugegen,
Hörte die Töchterchen singen, und war entzückt und in Laune.
Manches verstand ich nicht, was in den Liedern gesagt war;
Aber ich hörte viel von Pamina, viel von Tamino,
Und ich wollte doch auch nicht stumm sein! Sobald sie geendet,
Fragt ich dem Texte nach, und nach den beiden Personen.
Alle schwiegen darauf und lächelten; aber der Vater
Sagte: Nicht wahr, mein Freund, er kennt nur Adam und Eva?
Niemand hielt sich alsdann, und laut auf lachten die Mädchen,
Laut auf lachten die Knaben, es hielt den Bauch sich der Alte.
Fallen ließ ich den Hut vor Verlegenheit, und das Gekicher
Dauerte fort und fort, so viel sie auch sangen und spielten.
Und ich eilte beschämt und verdrießlich wieder nach Hause,
Hängte den Rock in den Schrank, und zog die Haare herunter
Mit den Fingern, und schwur nicht mehr zu betreten die Schwelle.
Und ich hatte wohl recht; denn eitel sind sie und lieblos,
Und ich höre, noch heiß ich bei ihnen immer Tamino.

Da versetzte die Mutter: Du solltest, Hermann, so lange
Mit den Kindern nicht zürnen; denn Kinder sind sie ja sämtlich.
Minchen fürwahr ist gut, und war dir immer gewogen;
Neulich fragte sie noch nach dir. Die solltest du wählen!

Was, I distinctly remember, on Easter Sunday, and I had
Carefully dressed in the fashionable coat I had recently
bought, (which
Hangs now forlorn in the closet) and combed up my hair
like the others.
When I came in they were giggling, but not at me, I was certain. 220
Mina was at the piano, and their old father was present,
List'ning with joy to the songs of his daughters, quite happy
and cheerful.
I could not understand very much of the text they were singing,
But I did hear a lot about Pamina, Tamino.
Naturally I did not want to be silent, so when they had finished
I asked what was the text, and who were the characters mentioned.
All were silent at this, but they smiled, and the father responded:
'Tell me, my friend, you're acquainted only with Eve and
with Adam?'
Then they could hold back no longer: the girls simply hooted
with laughter;
Loud laughed also the lads, and the father was holding 230
his stomach.
I was embarrassed and dropped my hat on the floor, and the
giggling
Went on, even through singing and playing I heard it continue.
And I went home as fast as I could in disgrace and vexation,
Hung the new coat in the closet, and mussed up my hair with
my fingers,
Swearing that never again would I ever set foot on their threshold.
And, indeed, I was right, for they are conceited and hateful,
And, as I hear, they are always referring to me as Tamino."

Then his mother replied to him: "Hermann, you should
not be angry
Now at them any longer, for they are no better than children.
Mina is nice, to be sure, and was always inclined in your favor. 240
Lately she asked how you were. I believe it is she you should marry."

Da versetzte bedenklich der Sohn: Ich weiß nicht, es prägte
Jener Verdruß sich so tief bei mir ein, ich möchte fürwahr nicht
Sie am Klaviere mehr sehn und ihre Liedchen vernehmen.

Doch der Vater fuhr auf und sprach die zornigen Worte:
Wenig Freud erleb ich an dir! Ich sagt es doch immer,
Als du zu Pferden nur und Lust nur bezeigtest zum Acker:
Was ein Knecht schon verrichtet des wohlbegüterten Mannes,
Tust du; indessen muß der Vater des Sohnes entbehren,
Der ihm zur Ehre doch auch vor andern Bürgern sich zeigte.
Und so täuschte mich früh mit leerer Hoffnung die Mutter
Wenn in der Schule das Lesen und Schreiben und Lernen, dir niemals
Wie den andern gelang und du immer der unterste saßest.
Freilich! das kommt daher, wenn Ehrgefühl nicht im Busen
Eines Jünglinges lebt, und wenn er nicht höher hinauf will.
Hätte mein Vater gesorgt für mich, so wie ich für dich tat,
Mich zur Schule gesendet und mir die Lehrer gehalten,
Ja, ich wäre was anders als Wirt zum Goldenen Löwen.

Aber der Sohn stand auf und nahte sich schweigend der Türe,
Langsam und ohne Geräusch; allein der Vater, entrüstet,
Rief ihm nach: So gehe nur hin! ich kenne den Trotzkopf!
Geh und führe fortan die Wirtschaft, daß ich nicht schelte;
Aber denke nur nicht, du wollest ein bäurisches Mädchen
Je mir bringen ins Haus, als Schwiegertochter, die Trulle!
Lange hab ich gelebt und weiß mit Menschen zu handeln,
Weiß zu bewirten die Herren und Frauen, daß sie zufrieden
Von mir weggehn; ich weiß den Fremden gefällig zu schmeicheln.

Hermann reluctantly answered: "Why, really, that mortification
Made such distressing impression on me that I would be happy
If I never again heard her sing or play the piano."

But then his father sprang up and spoke these words in
great anger:
"Little delight do you give me! I always have known it and
said it:
When you displayed inclination only for horses and grainfields.
Work which the servants of propertied men perform for their
wages,
You do! Meanwhile your father dispenses with honor which only
You could provide by making appearance in public. Your mother
Cheated me early with vain expectations, when in your schooldays
Such things as reading and writing and learning would never
go into
Your head, like other lads, and always you sat at the bottom.
Naturally that comes about when no spark of ambition exists in
Mind or heart of a youth who does *not* want to rise any higher.
Had my father provided for me as for you I provided,
Sent me to school and employed the best teachers for private
instruction,
I would have been something more than the innkeeper here at
the Lion."

But his son then arose and wordlessly walked to the doorway,
Slowly, without any noise, but his father indignantly shouted: 260
"All right—just go! I know you are stubborn and terribly wilful.
Go, and manage the farming henceforward, and don't make
me angry.
But don't suppose I'll ever permit you to bring as your wife here
Just any girl from a farm: I'll simply not have her, the hussy!
Long have I lived and well I know how to deal with the people,
How to be friendly with guests, and how I can give satisfaction.
Also I know how to flatter a stranger with courteous treatment.

Aber so soll mir denn auch ein Schwiegertöchterchen endlich
Wiederbegegnen und so mir die viele Mühe versüßen;
Spielen soll sie mir auch das Klavier; es sollen die schönsten,
Besten Leute der Stadt sich mit Vergnügen versammeln,
Wie es sonntags geschieht im Hause des Nachbars. Da drückte
Leise der Sohn auf die Klinke, und so verließ er die Stube.

III

THALIA

Die Bürger

Also entwich der bescheidene Sohn der heftigen Rede;
Aber der Vater fuhr in der Art fort, wie er begonnen:
Was im Menschen nicht ist, kommt auch nicht aus ihm, und schwerlich
Wird mich des herzlichsten Wunsches Erfüllung jemals erfreuen,
Daß der Sohn dem Vater nicht gleich sei, sondern ein Beßrer.
Denn was wäre das Haus, was wäre die Stadt, wenn nicht immer
Jeder gedächte mit Lust zu erhalten und zu erneuen,
Und zu verbessern auch, wie die Zeit uns lehrt und das Ausland!
Soll doch nicht als ein Pilz der Mensch dem Boden entwachsen,
Und verfaulen geschwind an dem Platze, der ihn erzeugt hat,
Keine Spur nachlassend von seiner lebendigen Wirkung!
Sieht man am Hause doch gleich so deutlich, wes Sinnes der Herr sei,

That is the way I expect any daughter-in-law to requite me,
So that the labor of so many years will be softened and
sweetened.
She must be able to play the piano, and all the élite and 270
Best of the townsfolk will come to enjoy it, just as it happens
Sundays, there in the house of our neighbor." Then, gently,
did Hermann
Push on the latch, and, opening the door, go out of the parlor.

III

THALIA

The Citizens

Thus the diffident Hermann escaped from this violent
language.
But his father continued to speak in the way he had started:
"That which a man does not have cannot be drawn from
him either.
Hardly will ever my dearest desire achieve its fulfillment:
Namely, that Hermann will be not like his father, but better.
What indeed would become of city or house unless always
Everyone cheerfully strove to preserve and renew and make
better,
Even as modern times and examples in other lands
teach us.
Man is not after all predestined to grow like a
mushroom
Up from the ground, then suddenly rot in the place that 10
produced him,
Leaving no vestige behind of the life he has led and its outcome.
Clearly one sees in a house the nature and soul of
its owner,

Wie man, das Städtchen betretend, die Obrigkeiten beurteilt.
Denn wo die Türme verfallen und Mauern, wo in den Gräben
Unrat sich häufet, und Unrat auf allen Gassen herumliegt,
Wo der Stein aus der Fuge sich rückt und nicht wieder gesetzt wird,
Wo der Balken verfault und das Haus vergeblich die neue
Unterstützung erwartet: der Ort ist übel regieret.
Denn wo nicht immer von oben die Ordnung und Reinlichkeit wirket,
Da gewöhnet sich leicht der Bürger zu schmutzigem Saumsal,
Wie der Bettler sich auch an lumpige Kleider gewöhnet.
Darum hab ich gewünscht, es solle sich Hermann auf Reisen
Bald begeben, und sehn zum wenigsten Straßburg und Frankfurt.
Und das freundliche Mannheim, das gleich und heiter gebaut ist.
Denn wer die Städte gesehn, die großen und reinlichen, ruht nicht,
Künftig die Vaterstadt selbst, so klein sie auch sei, zu verzieren.
Lobt nicht der Fremde bei uns die ausgebesserten Tore,
Und den geweißten Turm und die wohlerneuerte Kirche?
Rühmt nicht jeder das Pflaster? die wasserreichen, verdeckten,
Wohlverteilten Kanäle, die Nutzen und Sicherheit bringen,
Daß dem Feuer sogleich beim ersten Ausbruch gewehrt sei,
Ist das nicht alles geschehn seit jenem schrecklichen Brande?
Bauherr war ich sechsmal im Rat, und habe mir Beifall,
Habe mir herzlichen Dank von guten Bürgern verdienet,
Was ich angab, emsig betrieben, und so auch die Anstalt
Redlicher Männer vollführt, die sie unvollendet verließen.
So kam endlich die Lust in jedes Mitglied des Rates.
Alle bestreben sich jetzt, und schon ist der neue Chausseebau
Fest beschlossen, der uns mit der großen Straße verbindet.

As, when one enters a city, he judges its government's nature.
For, where the steeples and walls are in ruins, and ditches
are full of
Rubbish, and rubbish is scattered all over the alleys and
roads, where
Masonry crumbles to bits and nobody ever repairs it;
Beams of old dwellings rot slowly but surely away, and the houses
Vainly await new supports; such a city is shockingly governed.
For unless always the government demonstrates order and neatness,
Citizens easily fall into negligent, slovenly habits, 20
Just as the beggar accustoms his person to raggedy clothing.
Thus have I wished that my Hermann soon would think
about travel,
Journey to Strassburg and Frankfurt at least, or to beautiful
Mannheim,
Which is constructed so evenly, and has such a charming
appearance.
For whoever has visited clean and sizable cities
Soon would adorn the place of his birth, be it ever so little.
Do not strangers admire the way we have mended our gateway?
How we have painted our steeple? And also the church
renovation.
Does not everyone praise our excellent paving? Our water
System, abundant, and covered, and fairly distributed, bringing 30
Safety and practical use in prevention of fire at its outbreak?
All of this was achieved since the time of the great conflagration.
Six terms of service as building commissioner brought me
great credit;
Merited thanks were returned to me by our excellent townsmen.
What I suggested I zealously fostered, and also the plans which
Other competent men had not finished I brought to conclusion.
My example of zeal has inspired them all on the council.
All are eagerly active at present; already construction
On the new road to the highway has met with the council's
approval.

Aber ich fürchte nur sehr, so wird die Jugend nicht handeln!
Denn die einen, sie denken auf Lust und vergänglichen Putz nur;
Andere hocken zu Haus und brüten hinter dem Ofen.
Und das fürcht ich, ein solcher wird Hermann immer mir bleiben.

Und es versetzte sogleich die gute verständige Mutter:
Immer bist du doch, Vater, so ungerecht gegen den Sohn! und
So wird am wenigsten dir dein Wunsch des Guten erfüllet.
Denn wir können die Kinder nach unserem Sinne nicht formen;
So wie Gott sie uns gab, so muß man sie haben und lieben,
Sie erziehen aufs beste und jeglichen lassen gewähren.
Denn der eine hat die, die anderen andere Gaben;
Jeder braucht sie, und jeder ist doch nur auf eigene Weise
Gut und glücklich. Ich lasse mir meinen Hermann nicht schelten;
Denn, ich weiß es, er ist der Güter, die er dereinst erbt,
Wert und ein trefflicher Wirt, ein Muster Bürgern und Bauern,
Und im Rate gewiß, ich seh es voraus, nicht der Letzte.
Aber täglich mit Schelten und Tadeln hemmst du dem Armen
Allen Mut in der Brust, so wie du es heute getan hast.
Und sie verließ die Stube sogleich, und eilte dem Sohn nach,
Daß sie ihn irgendwo fänd und ihn mit gütigen Worten
Wieder erfreute; denn er, der treffliche Sohn, er verdient' es.

Lächelnd sagte darauf, sobald sie hinweg war, der Vater:
Sind doch ein wunderlich Volk die Weiber, so wie die Kinder!
Jedes lebet so gern nach seinem eignen Belieben,
Und man sollte hernach nur immer loben und streicheln.

But I am sorely afraid that the new generation will not be 40
Half as active as we are. Some can think only of pleasure,
Clothing, adornment, while others sit lazily home by the fireplace.
This it is which I fear: a fate like this for my Hermann."

Promptly, with vigor, the good intelligent mother responded:
"Father, why are you speaking so often unjustly of Hermann?
Thus you can never achieve your wishes' dearest fulfillment.
Children cannot be formed exactly as we would like them.
Just as God gave them to us we must cherish them always,
and love them,
Raise them the best way we can, and leave them free to develop.
Some have one sort of talents, and others are differently gifted; 50
Everyone uses his talents, and everyone finds satisfaction,
Only in one way, his own. My Hermann must not be scolded:
For I know he is worthy of all the goods we shall leave him.
He is an excellent landlord, a model for farmers and
townsmen.
And in the council, I think, he will not be the last to be
heard from.
You, with your carping and nagging, hinder the lad and inhibit
Thoroughly all his self-confidence, just as today you were doing."
So she departed at once from the room to search for young
Hermann,
Hoping to find him somewhere and cheer him with kindly
affection,
For she believed that her excellent son was deserving of comfort. 60

Smiling the father remarked, as soon as the mother had left
them:
"Women in truth are very peculiar, and much like their children.
Each of them likes to manage affairs in accord with her
judgment,
Then in the end they demand from us men caresses and praises.

Einmal für allemal gilt das wahre Sprüchlein der Alten:
Wer nicht vorwärts geht, der kommt zurücke! So bleibt es.

Und es versetzte darauf der Apotheker bedächtig:
Gerne geb ich es zu, Herr Nachbar, und sehe mich immer
Selbst nach dem Besseren um, wofern es nicht teuer doch neu ist;
Aber hilft es fürwahr, wenn man nicht die Fülle des Gelds hat,
Tätig und rührig zu sein und innen und außen zu bessern?
Nur zu sehr ist der Bürger beschränkt; das Gute vermag er
Nicht zu erlangen, wenn er es kennt. Zu schwach ist sein Beutel,
Das Bedürfnis zu groß; so wird er immer gehindert.
Manches hätt ich getan; allein wer scheut nicht die Kosten
Solcher Verändrung, besonders in diesen gefährlichen Zeiten!
Lange lachte mir schon mein Haus im modischen Kleidchen,
Lange glänzten durchaus mit großen Scheiben die Fenster;
Aber wer tut dem Kaufmann es nach, der bei seinem Vermögen
Auch die Wege noch kennt, auf welchen das Beste zu haben?
Seht nur das Haus an da drüben, das neue! Wie prächtig in grünen
Feldern die Stukkatur der weißen Schnörkel sich ausnimmt!
Groß sind die Tafeln der Fenster; wie glänzen und spiegeln die Scheiben,
Daß verdunkelt stehn die übrigen Häuser des Marktes!
Und doch waren die unsern gleich nach dem Brande die schönsten,
Die Apotheke zum Engel, sowie der Goldene Löwe.
So war mein Garten auch in der ganzen Gegend berühmt, und
Jeder Reisende stand und sah durch die roten Staketen
Nach den Bettlern von Stein, und nach den farbigen Zwergen.
Wem ich den Kaffee dann gar in dem herrlichen Grottenwerk reichte,

Once and for all I remind you: how true is the famous old adage:
'He who will not advance, must recede'—and that ends the matter."

Then the druggist replied to his host in deliberate manner:
"Glad I am to admit the truth of the saying, good neighbor.
Always I look for the better, the new, if it's not too expensive.
But what good does it do, if you have no abundance of money, 70
Always to be on the go, improving the inside and outside?
Townsfolk are closely restricted; they never acquire things of value,
Even though these be familiar—their purses are empty
and useless.
Since their needs are excessive, their power is always restricted.
Much I would gladly have done, but I could not bear the expenses.
Of such improvements, especially when life is beset with such
danger!
Long would my house have been smiling at me in its stylish
adornment,
Long would my windows with lengthier, wider panes have
been gleaming;
But can anyone equal the merchant, who, with his fortune,
Also is sure of the ways to acquire those precious possessions? 80
Just take a look at his house over there, the new one; how brightly
There against the green panels the stucco's white convolutions
Shine; how large are the casements! The window panes sparkle
and cast in
Shadow the rest of the houses which stand at the edge of the
market.
But just after the fire you and I had the best of the houses:
Pharmacy Archangel Michael, the Inn of the Gold-painted Lion!
Likewise my garden was famed in the neighborhood; every
stranger
Stood at the gate and peered through the pickets of red at the
plaster
Beggars and dwarves in all their interesting, colorful splendor.
When the coffee was served inside the magnificent grotto 90

Das nun freilich verstaubt und halb verfallen mir dasteht,
Der erfreute sich hoch des farbig schimmernden Lichtes
Schöngeordneter Muscheln; und mit geblendetem Auge
Schaute der Kenner selbst den Bleiglanz und die Korallen.
Eben so ward in dem Saale die Malerei auch bewundert,
Wo die geputzten Herren und Damen im Garten spazieren
Und mit spitzigen Fingern die Blumen reichen und halten.
Ja, wer sähe das jetzt nur noch an! Ich gehe verdrießlich
Kaum mehr hinaus; denn alles soll anders sein und geschmackvoll,
Wie sie's heißen, und weiß die Latten und hölzernen Bänke.
Alles ist einfach und glatt; nicht Schnitzwerk oder Vergoldung
Will man mehr, und es kostet das fremde Holz nun am meisten.
Nun, ich wär es zufrieden, mir auch was Neues zu schaffen;
Auch zu gehn mit der Zeit, und oft zu verändern den Hausrat;
Aber es fürchtet sich jeder, auch nur zu rücken das kleinste,
Denn wer vermöchte wohl jetzt die Arbeitsleute zu zahlen?
Neulich kam mir's in Sinn, den Engel Michael wieder,
Der mir die Offizin bezeichnet, vergolden zu lassen,
Und den greulichen Drachen, der ihm zu Füßen sich windet;
Aber ich ließ ihn verbräunt, wie er ist; mich schreckte die Fordrung.

(Which to be sure is now moldering fast, and is almost in ruins)
Strangers were deeply impressed by the radiant play of the light in
All of the shells, so neatly arranged; and with thunderstruck wonder
Even the connoisseur admired the galena and corals.
Likewise there in the parlor the murals evoked admiration,
Where the ladies and gallants in costume walk through the garden
And, with tapering fingers, hand each other the flowers.
Yes! But who now would look at such things? O, I am annoyed and
Scarcely ever go out there; for things are supposed to be diff'rent:
('Tasteful' they call it!) Lattices, benches of wood must be always 100
Painted the color of white, and all must be simple and smooth, and
Carving and gilt are unwanted, and wood from abroad is expensive.
Well, it would satisfy me to buy something new for my household,
Just to keep up with the times and often to change my arrangements.
Yet we seem to be wary of making the least alteration:
Who could pay the expense of the labor for such renovations?
Lately I had the idea of gilding the Archangel Michael,
Who is the sign of my business, as well as the frightening dragon
Writhing impaled at the feet of the angel, but I was forced to
Leave him tarnished and brown, as he is—the estimate scared me." 110

IV

EUTERPE

Mutter und Sohn

Also sprachen die Männer sich unterhaltend. Die Mutter
Ging indessen, den Sohn erst vor dem Hause zu suchen,
Auf der steinernen Bank, wo sein gewöhnlicher Sitz war.
Als sie daselbst ihn nicht fand, so ging sie, im Stalle zu
schauen,
Ob er die herrlichen Pferde, die Hengste, selber besorgte,
Die er als Fohlen gekauft und die er niemand vertraute.
Und es sagte der Knecht: Er ist in den Garten gegangen.
Da durchschritt sie behende die langen doppelten Höfe,
Ließ die Ställe zurück und die wohlgezimmerten Scheunen,
Trat in den Garten, der weit bis an die Mauern des Städtchens
Reichte, schritt ihn hindurch, und freute sich jegliches
Wachstums,
Stellte die Stützen zurecht, auf denen beladen die Äste
Ruhten des Apfelbaums, wie des Birnbaums lastende
Zweige,
Nahm gleich einige Raupen vom kräftig strotzenden Kohl
weg;
Denn ein geschäftiges Weib tut keine Schritte vergebens.
Also war sie ans Ende des langen Gartens gekommen,
Bis zur Laube mit Geisblatt bedeckt; nicht fand sie den
Sohn da,

IV

EUTERPE

Mother and Son

Thus, in light conversation, the men spoke one to another.
Meanwhile the mother went out to look for her son by the
housefront,
There on the bench made of stone, which he was accustomed
to sit on.
When she found him not there she went to look in the stable,
Where he might be, grooming his stallions, incomparable horses,
Which he had bought when just foaled, and which he entrusted
to no one.
But she was told by the servant: "Hermann has gone to the
garden."
Then she rapidly crossed the long double courtyard before her,
Leaving the stables behind, and the carefully carpentered haybarn,
Entered the garden, which stretched right out to the walls
of the city; 10
Took her way through it, observing with pleasure the growth of
her projects;
Fixed the supports of the appletree, on which the branches
were resting,
Heavily laden, as well as the groaning boughs of the peartree;
Took away cankerous worms from the flourishing leaves of
the cabbage;
For an industrious woman is never idle a moment.
Thus she had come to the end of the garden, extensive and
fruitful,
Up to the arbor, covered with woodbine, nor there could she
find him,

Ebensowenig als sie bis jetzt ihn im Garten erblickte.
Aber nur angelehnt war das Pförtchen, das aus der Laube,
Aus besonderer Gunst, durch die Mauer des Städtchens gebrochen
Hatte der Ahnherr einst, der würdige Burgemeister.
Und so ging sie bequem den trocknen Graben hinüber,
Wo an der Straße sogleich der wohlumzäunete Weinberg
Aufstieg steileren Pfads, die Fläche zur Sonne gekehret.
Auch den schritt sie hinauf, und freute der Fülle der Trauben
Sich im Steigen, die kaum sich unter den Blättern verbargen.
Schattig war und bedeckt der hohe mittlere Laubgang,
Den man auf Stufen erstieg von unbehauenen Platten.
Und es hingen herein Gutedel und Muskateller,
Rötlich blaue daneben von ganz besonderer Größe,
Alle mit Fleiße gepflanzt, der Gäste Nachtisch zu zieren.
Aber den übrigen Berg bedeckten einzelne Stöcke,
Kleinere Trauben tragend, von denen der köstliche Wein kommt.
Also schritt sie hinauf, sich schon des Herbstes erfreuend
Und des festlichen Tags, an dem die Gegend im Jubel
Trauben lieset und tritt, und den Most in die Fässer versammelt,
Feuerwerke des Abends von allen Orten und Enden
Leuchten und knallen, und so der Ernten schönste geehrt wird.
Doch unruhiger ging sie, nachdem sie dem Sohne gerufen
Zwei- auch dreimal, und nur das Echo vielfach zurückkam,
Das von den Türmen der Stadt, ein sehr geschwätziges, herklang.
Ihn zu suchen war ihr so fremd; er entfernte sich niemals
Weit, er sagt' es ihr denn, um zu verhüten die Sorge
Seiner liebenden Mutter und ihre Furcht vor dem Unfall.
Aber sie hoffte noch stets, ihn doch auf dem Wege zu finden;

Just as she had not been able so far to discover him any
Place in the garden. The gate was, however, only ajar, which
Once, as a favor, a worthy progenitor, mayor of the city, 20
Built in the wall long ago, as an exit out of the arbor.
So she conveniently passed through the moat, now empty of water,
Where from the edge of the road the vineyard, enclosed with
precision,
Rose by a steeper ascent and presented its face to the sunshine.
This was the path she ascended, observing with deep satisfaction
All the abundance of grapes, which were scarcely concealed by
the foliage.
Shaded, protected by leaves was the passage which ran through
the middle,
Reached by a steep flight of steps, made of stone, untouched
by a mason.
Here hung the chasselas grapes, and muscatel also in fulness,
Reddish blue grapes beside them of most unusual largeness. 30
All of them planted with care to sweeten dessert for the patrons.
Over the rest of the hill individual grapevines were growing,
Bearing the smaller varieties, whence the most exquisite
wine comes.
So then she strode up the hill, rejoicing in prospects of autumn,
And of the festival day when the jubilant neighbors assemble,
Gath'ring and treading the grapes, and collecting new wine in
the barrels,
Everywhere, in the evening, fireworks exploding and shining,
Gleaming high in the sky to honor the fairest of harvests;
But she was troubled in spirit, after she called to her son, not
Once, but two or three times, and received but an echo for answer, 40
Which in chattering tones the town threw back from its towers.
Searching for him was a new thing for her, for never before had
Hermann gone far from his home without saying where he
was going,
So as to keep from his mother concern that he suffer misfortune.
But she hoped all the same to find him soon on the pathway,

Denn die Türen, die untre, sowie die obre, des Weinbergs
Standen gleichfalls offen. Und so nun trat sie ins Feld ein,
Das mit weiter Fläche den Rücken des Hügels bedeckte.
Immer noch wandelte sie auf eigenem Boden, und freute
Sich der eigenen Saat und des herrlich nickenden Kornes,
Das mit goldener Kraft sich im ganzen Felde bewegte.
Zwischen den Äckern schritt sie hindurch, auf dem Raine, den Fußpfad,
Hatte den Birnbaum im Auge, den großen, der auf dem Hügel
Stand, die Grenze der Felder, die ihrem Hause gehörten.
Wer ihn gepflanzt, man konnt es nicht wissen. Er war in der Gegend
Weit und breit gesehn, und berühmt die Früchte des Baumes.
Unter ihm pflegten die Schnitter des Mahls sich zu freuen am Mittag,
Und die Hirten des Viehs in seinem Schatten zu warten;
Bänke fanden sie da von rohen Steinen und Rasen.
Und sie irrete nicht; dort saß ihr Hermann und ruhte,
Saß mit dem Arme gestützt und schien in die Gegend zu schauen
Jenseits, nach dem Gebirg, er kehrte der Mutter den Rücken.
Sachte schlich sie hinan, und rührt' ihm leise die Schulter.
Und er wandte sich schnell; da sah sie ihm Tränen im Auge.

Mutter, sagt' er betroffen, ihr überrascht mich! Und eilig
Trocknet' er ab die Träne, der Jüngling edlen Gefühles.
Wie? du weinest, mein Sohn? versetzte die Mutter betroffen:
Daran kenn ich dich nicht! ich habe das niemals erfahren!

Since the doors of the vineyard, the upper as well as the lower,
Also were open. And so she presently entered the grainfield,
Which in its spacious expanse extended over the hillside.
Still all the ground was her own, over which she continued to wander.
Pleased with the crops she had sown, with the grain ears splendidly waving, 50
Stirring in golden magnificence over the face of the grainfield.
Through the fields then she passed, on the footpath which served as a border,
Aiming straight for the peartree, the large one that stood on the hill and
Marked the boundary and end of the fields which belonged to the family.
Nobody knew who had planted it. Far and wide in the landscape
People could see it; the fruit of the tree was also quite famous.
Under its branches the mowers, resting, would eat in the noontime;
Herdsmen were much in the habit of tending their flocks in its shadow,
Sitting on benches of stone and on grass at the foot of the peartree.
Nor was the mother mistaken. There sat Hermann and rested, 60
Leaning back on his arms; he seemed to look into the distance,
There where the mountain range stood; his face turned away from his mother.
Softly she stole up behind him and laid her hand on his shoulder.
Swiftly he turned full around, and she saw the traces of weeping.

"Mother," he said in embarrassment, "I am astonished to see you."
Quickly the high-minded youth wiped away the tears that had fallen.
"What, are you weeping, my son?" said his mother, likewise embarrassed;
"This seems a strange thing to me; I have never known you to do it.

Sag, was beklemmt dir das Herz? was treibt dich, einsam zu sitzen
Unter dem Birnbaum hier? was bringt dir Tränen ins Auge?

Und es nahm sich zusammen der treffliche Jüngling, und sagte:
Wahrlich, dem ist kein Herz im ehernen Busen, der jetzo
Nicht die Not der Menschen, der umgetriebnen, empfindet;
Dem ist kein Sinn in dem Haupte, der nicht um sein eigenes Wohl sich
Und um des Vaterlands Wohl in diesen Tagen bekümmert.
Was ich heute gesehn und gehört, das rührte das Herz mir;
Und nun ging ich heraus, und sah die herrliche weite
Landschaft, die sich vor uns in fruchtbaren Hügeln umher schlingt;
Sah die goldene Frucht den Garben entgegen sich neigen,
Und ein reichliches Obst uns volle Kammern versprechen.
Aber, ach! wie nah ist der Feind! Die Fluten des Rheines
Schützen uns zwar; doch ach! was sind nun Fluten und Berge
Jenem schrecklichen Volke, das wie ein Gewitter daherzieht!
Denn sie rufen zusammen aus allen Enden die Jugend,
Wie das Alter, und dringen gewaltig vor, und die Menge
Scheut den Tod nicht; es dringt gleich nach der Menge die Menge.
Ach! und ein Deutscher wagt in seinem Hause zu bleiben?
Hofft vielleicht zu entgehen dem alles bedrohenden Unfall?
Liebe Mutter, ich sag euch, am heutigen Tage verdrießt mich,
Daß man mich neulich entschuldigt, als man die Streitenden auslas
Aus den Bürgern. Fürwahr! ich bin der einzige Sohn nur,
Und die Wirtschaft ist groß, und wichtig unser Gewerbe;
Aber wär ich nicht besser, zu widerstehen da vorne
An der Grenze, als hier zu erwarten Elend und Knechtschaft?

Tell me, what weighs on your heart? What makes you sit by the
pear tree
Here all alone, and whatever has caused this unusual weeping?" 70

Then the excellent youth plucked up his courage and
answered:
"Truly there can be no heart in that bosom of brass of the man who
Feels not a qualm when he sees how the wandering exiles are
suff'ring;
He has no sense in his head who is worried by neither his own weal
Nor by the weal of his country, now so gravely imperilled.
That which today I have seen and have heard has shaken my
spirit.
Then I went out and beheld the magnificent landscape around us,
Stretching away at our feet in fruitful valleys and hillsides;
Saw the golden harvest of sheaves, bending down to the earth in
Plenteous splendor, and fruits in abundance, to fill up our 80
cellars.
But, alas, how close are our foemen! The floods of the Rhine still
Guard us, of course, but what sort of protection can rivers and
mountains
Give us against such a terrible people, whose march is a tempest.
For they are calling their young men and old men from every
direction,
Moving mightily forward; the multitudes seem unaffrighted
Even by death, for they quickly fill up the ranks of the fallen.
How can a German presume to sit quiet at home, or to hope for
Possible rescue from imminent threats of death and disaster?
Mother, I tell you, today I am vexed that I was exempted,
Recently, when the levy of soldiers was raised in our city. 90
Yes, it is true that I am the only son of my parents,
And that our business is large and our occupation important,
But would I not do better to stand and fight at the border,
Rather than wait for bondage and misery here with my parents?

Ja, mir hat es der Geist gesagt, und im innersten Busen
Regt sich Mut und Begier, dem Vaterlande zu leben
Und zu sterben, und andern ein würdiges Beispiel zu geben.
Wahrlich, wäre die Kraft der deutschen Jugend beisammen,
An der Grenze, verbündet, nicht nachzugeben den Fremden,
O, sie sollten uns nicht den herrlichen Boden betreten,
Und vor unseren Augen die Früchte des Landes verzehren,
Nicht den Männern gebieten und rauben Weiber und
Mädchen!
Sehet! Mutter, mir ist im tiefsten Herzen beschlossen,
Bald zu tun und gleich, was recht mir deucht und verständig;
Denn wer lange bedenkt, der wählt nicht immer das beste.
Sehet, ich werde nicht wieder nach Hause kehren!
Von hier aus
Geh ich gerad in die Stadt, und übergebe den Kriegern
Diesen Arm und dies Herz, dem Vaterlande zu dienen.
Sage der Vater alsdann, ob nicht der Ehre Gefühl mir
Auch den Busen belebt, und ob ich nicht höher hinauf will!

Da versetzte bedeutend die gute verständige Mutter,
Stille Tränen vergießend, sie kamen ihr leichtlich ins Auge:
Sohn, was hat sich in dir verändert und deinem Gemüte,
Daß du zu deiner Mutter nicht redest, wie gestern und immer
Offen und frei, und sagst was deinen Wünschen gemäß ist?
Hörte jetzt ein dritter dich reden, er würde fürwahr dich
Höchlich loben und deinen Entschluß als den edelsten
preisen,
Durch dein Wort verführt und deine bedeutenden Reden.
Doch ich tadle dich nur; denn sieh, ich kenne dich besser.
Du verbirgst dein Herz und hast ganz andre Gedanken.

Yes, I know I am right; I can sense in the depths of my spirit
Courage and eagerness stirring, to live for my country, and even,
If it be needful, to die, as a worthy example to others.
If the youth of the country would stand in strength at the border,
Firmly bound in good faith that they never will yield to these
strangers,
Then they would never set foot within our magnificent country, 100
Never consume, while we watch them, the fruits of our land and
our labor,
Never would bully our men, nor abscond with our girls and our
women.
Mother, please understand that my heart has made its decision
Now to perform what I think is a right and intelligent action.
For, a person who hesitates long cannot always be sure of
Making the choice that is wisest. So, mother, I will not go
home with
You now. Straight to the city I'll go and enlist in the army,
Give to the soldiers my strength and my courage to serve my
dear country.
Let then my father declare that the noblest feelings of honor
Do not dwell in my bosom or that ambition is lacking!" 110

Then there responded with meaning the worthy intelligent mother,
Quietly shedding her tears, which abundantly flowed, in her sorrow:
"Son, what change has occurred that has utterly altered your spirit?
That to your mother you speak not at all in the usual manner,
Openly, freely, and frankly, and say what you really are wishing;
If another should hear you, indeed, he would praise you most
highly,
Hailing your noble resolve as the worthiest, finest decision,
Duped by your eloquent words, and deceived by your passionate
language.
I, on the other hand, blame you for this, for I know you much better;
You are concealing your heart and are thinking something 120
quite different.

Denn ich weiß es, dich ruft nicht die Trommel, nicht die Trompete,
Nicht begehrst du zu scheinen in der Montur vor den Mädchen;
Denn es ist deine Bestimmung, so wacker und brav du auch sonst bist,
Wohl zu verwahren das Haus und stille das Feld zu besorgen.
Darum sage mir frei: was dringt dich zu dieser Entschließung?

Ernsthaft sagte der Sohn: Ihr irret, Mutter. Ein Tag ist
Nicht dem anderen gleich. Der Jüngling reifet zum Manne;
Besser im stillen reift er zur Tat oft, als im Geräusche
Wilden schwankenden Lebens, das manchen Jüngling verderbt hat.
Und so still ich auch bin und war, so hat in der Brust mir
Doch sich gebildet ein Herz, das Unrecht hasset und Unbill,
Und ich verstehe recht gut die weltlichen Dinge zu sondern;
Auch hat die Arbeit den Arm und die Füße mächtig gestärket.
Alles, fühl ich, ist wahr; ich darf es kühnlich behaupten.
Und doch tadelt ihr mich mit Recht, o Mutter, und habt mich
Auf halbwahren Worten ertappt und halber Verstellung.
Denn, gesteh ich es nur, nicht ruft die nahe Gefahr mich
Aus dem Hause des Vaters, und nicht der hohe Gedanke,
Meinem Vaterland hülfreich zu sein und schrecklich den Feinden.
Worte waren es nur, die ich sprach: sie sollten vor euch nur
Meine Gefühle verstecken, die mir das Herz zerreißen.
Und so laßt mich, o Mutter! Denn da ich vergebliche Wünsche
Hege im Busen, so mag auch mein Leben vergeblich dahin gehn.
Denn ich weiß es recht wohl: der einzelne schadet sich selber,

Well do I know you are summoned neither by drums nor by trumpets,
Nor are you eager to put on the uniform just to display your
Beauty to maidens; for, honest and good as you are, you are destined
Wisely to manage the house and to care for the land without fanfare.
Therefore, please tell me straight out: just why have you made this decision?"

Earnestly Hermann made answer: "You are mistaken, good mother.
One day is not like another. A youth matures into manhood.
Better to ripen to action in stillness than in the noisy
Tumult of aimless existence, that has ruined many a fellow!
Quiet though I may be, and always have been, in my bosom 130
Nevertheless there is beating a heart which despises injustice,
And I am easily able to separate good things from evil.
Also my labor has mightily strengthened my arms and my body.
All that I tell you I know to be true, and can boldly assert it;
Yet you are right to reprove me, dear mother; you really have caught me
Speaking but half of the truth, and halfway intending deception.
For, I am free to admit, it is not any danger that calls me
Out of the house of my father, nor is it the glorious plan of
Helping my country and fright'ning the enemy, far from her borders;
Words, nothing more, did I speak; for I wanted to keep you from knowing 140
What I actually felt, and how deeply my spirit was troubled.
Leave me, I beg you, dear mother! For since in my spirit I cherish
Wishes I cannot fulfill, let my life be without its fulfillment.
For (and I know this so well) when a man gives himself to a cause, he

Der sich hingibt, wenn sich nicht alle zum Ganzen bestreben.

Fahre nur fort, so sagte darauf die verständige Mutter,
Alles mir zu erzählen, das Größte wie das Geringste;
Denn die Männer sind heftig, und denken nur immer das Letzte,
Und die Hindernis treibt die Heftigen leicht von dem Wege;
Aber ein Weib ist geschickt, auf Mittel zu denken, und wandelt
Auch den Umweg, geschickt zu ihrem Zweck zu gelangen.
Sage mir alles daher, warum du so heftig bewegt bist,
Wie ich dich niemals gesehn, und das Blut dir wallt in den Adern,
Wider Willen die Träne dem Auge sich dringt zu entstürzen.

Da überließ sich dem Schmerze der gute Jüngling, und weinte,
Weinte laut an der Brust der Mutter, und sprach so erweichet:
Wahrlich! des Vaters Wort hat heute mich kränkend getroffen,
Das ich niemals verdient, nicht heut und keinen der Tage.
Denn die Eltern zu ehren war früh mein Liebstes, und niemand
Schien mir klüger zu sein und weiser, als die mich erzeugten
Und mit Ernst mir in dunkeler Zeit der Kindheit geboten.
Vieles hab ich fürwahr von meinen Gespielen geduldet,
Wenn sie mit Tücke mir oft den guten Willen vergalten;
Oftmals hab ich an ihnen nicht Wurf noch Streiche gerochen:
Aber spotteten sie mir den Vater aus, wenn er sonntags
Aus der Kirche kam mit würdig bedächtigem Schritte;
Lachten sie über das Band der Mütze, die Blumen des Schlafrocks,
Den er so stattlich trug und der erst heute verschenkt ward:

Only can damage himself, unless everyone else is devoted."

"Simply continue," rejoined his intelligent mother, "to tell me
All that your heart contains, the small things as well as the
big ones.
Men are very impetuous, quick to take violent action,
But any obstacle easily drives them aside from their pathway,
While a woman discreetly considers the means to her purpose, 150
Taking a sideroad if needful, to reach in the end her objective.
Tell me, dear son, the reason for being so mightily shaken.
Thus I have never beheld you! Your blood is impatiently coursing
Through all your veins, and you seem quite unable to hold back
your weeping."

Then the excellent youth, giving way to his sorrow,
began to
Weep out loud in his mother's embrace. And he said to her,
softened:
"Truly the words of my father today have offended my spirit.
They were deserved neither now nor ever before in my lifetime.
For to honor my parents was always my dearest objective.
Nobody seemed more discerning or wise than those who 160
begot me,
And who governed me during the difficult time of my childhood.
Much did I suffer in truth from the boys I usually played with,
When they responded with teasing to all the good I intended.
Often indeed I refrained from revenge against their
mistreatment.
But if they ridiculed father in coming from church of a
Sunday,
Laughed at his dignified gait or made fun of his cap with
its ribbons,
Mocked at the flowered décor of the housecoat, in which he
was always
Grandly parading, and which we disposed of only today, why,

Fürchterlich ballte sich gleich die Faust mir; mit grimmigem Wüten
Fiel ich sie an und schlug und traf, mit blindem Beginnen,
Ohne zu sehen wohin. Sie heulten mit blutigen Nasen,
Und entrissen sich kaum den wütenden Tritten und Schlägen.
Und so wuchs ich heran, um viel vom Vater zu dulden,
Der statt anderer mich gar oft mit Worten herum nahm,
Wenn bei Rat ihm Verdruß in der letzten Sitzung erregt ward;
Und ich büßte den Streit und die Ränke seiner Kollegen.
Oftmals habt ihr mich selbst bedauert; denn vieles ertrug ich,
Stets in Gedanken der Eltern von Herzen zu ehrende Wohltat,
Die nur sinnen, für uns zu mehren die Hab und die Güter,
Und sich selber manches entziehn, um zu sparen den Kindern.
Aber, ach! nicht das Sparen allein, um spät zu genießen,
Macht das Glück, es macht nicht das Glück der Haufe beim Haufen,
Nicht der Acker am Acker, so schön sich die Güter auch schließen.
Denn der Vater wird alt, und mit ihm altern die Söhne,
Ohne die Freude des Tags, und mit der Sorge für morgen.
Sagt mir, und schauet hinab, wie herrlich liegen die schönen,
Reichen Gebreite nicht da, und unten Weinberg und Gärten,
Dort die Scheunen und Ställe, die schöne Reihe der Güter;
Aber seh ich dann dort das Hinterhaus, wo an dem Giebel
Sich das Fenster uns zeigt von meinem Stübchen im Dache;
Denk ich die Zeiten zurück, wie manche Nacht ich den Mond schon
Dort erwartet und schon so manchen Morgen die Sonne,
Wenn der gesunde Schlaf mir nur wenige Stunden genügte:
Ach! da kommt mir so einsam vor, wie die Kammer, der Hof und

Then I would clench up my fists and attack them with savage
Passionate blows, with violence unseeing, regardless of danger. 170
Then they would wail, with their noses all bloody, and try to
escape as
Best as they could from the furious kicks and blows I delivered.
Thus then I came to my manhood, enduring the wrath of my
father,
Who let the guilty escape and let me feel the weight of his anger,
When, in the council's last session, somebody caused him vexation.
I had to pay for the strife and intrigues of the men on
the council.
Often you pitied me, then, for much did I suffer from father,
Always aware of the kindness of parents, who must be respected,
Since they only desire to increase their goods for their children,
Often depriving themselves, that their children may be all 180
the richer.
Ah! but frugality all by itself, with a view toward the future,
Never can bring us to happiness. Money, piled upon pile, or
Acre on acre can't do it, however fine their arrangement.
For the father grows old, and his sons grow old along with him,
Never enjoying the present and always concerned for the future.
Is it not so? Only look at our splendid and spacious estate there:
Rich is its lovely expanse! and look at the vineyards and gardens,
Stables and barns, and at all our possessions, so boundless and
fruitful.
But when I look at the rear of the house, just under the gable,
Where the window of my little room can be seen near 190
the housetop,
Then I think of the times in the night I have waited to see the
Moon coming up, and have sat there at daybreak to witness the
sunrise,
For in the vigor of health just a few moments' slumber
sufficed me.
Ah, then, my chamber seems lonely, and so do the farm and the
garden,

Garten, das herrliche Feld, das über die Hügel sich hinstreckt;
Alles liegt so öde vor mir: ich entbehre der Gattin.

Da antwortete drauf die gute Mutter verständig:
Sohn, mehr wünschest du nicht die Braut in die Kammer zu
führen,
Daß dir werde die Nacht zur schönen Hälfte des Lebens,
Und die Arbeit des Tags dir freier und eigener werde,
Als der Vater es wünscht und die Mutter. Wir haben dir
immer
Zugeredet, ja dich getrieben, ein Mädchen zu wählen.
Aber mir ist es bekannt, und jetzo sagt es das Herz mir:
Wenn die Stunde nicht kommt, die rechte, wenn nicht das
rechte
Mädchen zur Stunde sich zeigt, so bleibt das Wählen im
Weiten,
Und es wirket die Furcht die falsche zu greifen am meisten.
Soll ich dir sagen, mein Sohn, so hast du, ich glaube,
gewählet,
Denn dein Herz ist getroffen und mehr als gewöhnlich
empfindlich.
Sag es gerad nur heraus, denn mir schon sagt es die Seele:
Jenes Mädchen ist's, das vertriebene, die du gewählt hast.

Liebe Mutter, ihr sagt's! versetzte lebhaft der Sohn drauf.
Ja, sie ist's! und führ ich sie nicht als Braut mir nach Hause
Heute noch, ziehet sie fort, verschwindet vielleicht mir auf
immer
In der Verwirrung des Kriegs und im traurigen Hin- und
Herziehn.
Mutter, ewig umsonst gedeiht mir die reiche Besitzung
Dann vor Augen; umsonst sind künftige Jahre mir
fruchtbar.
Ja, das gewohnte Haus und der Garten ist mir zuwider;
Ach! und die Liebe der Mutter, sie selbst nicht tröstet den
Armen.

Even the glorious meadow extending over the hillside;
All my surroundings are dreary, for I have no wife to
console me."

Then his mother responded to this with deep understanding:
"Son, you cannot desire any more than your father and mother
That you may soon bring a wife to your chamber, so that the
night may
Be for you ever the fairest part of your life, and your daily 200
Labor thus may secure its freedom and meaning. How often
We have pled with you, begged you to choose a dear wife for
your bosom!
But I have always supposed, and my heart now confirms that
opinion:
If the right opportunity fails to appear, if the girl is
Also not right, or is not at hand at that moment, the choice is
Shelved an indefinite time, for one truly fears to choose
wrongly.
Shall I speak plainly, my boy? I believe your decision is taken:
For your heart seems affected, and you are uncommonly touchy.
Tell me now, straight from the shoulder, that which my spirit
has told me:
You have decided to marry the girl whom you saw with 210
the exiles."

"Mother dear, you are right!" responded Hermann with vigor,
"Yes, it is she! If I cannot this day bring her home as my
bride, if
Now she continues her journey, perhaps she will vanish forever
Out of my sight in the chaos of war and her sad emigration.
Mother, I tell you that all these possessions can never
contribute
Joy, however they flourish; in vain will my future be fruitful.
Yes, the house and the garden will be quite repellent, and even
Your love, mother, will never be able to comfort me, either.

Denn es löset die Liebe, das fühl ich, jegliche Bande,
Wenn sie die ihrigen knüpft; und nicht das Mädchen allein läßt
Vater und Mutter zurück, wenn sie dem erwähleten Mann folgt;
Auch der Jüngling, er weiß nichts mehr von Mutter und Vater,
Wenn er das Mädchen sieht, das einziggeliebte, davon ziehn.
Darum lasset mich gehn, wohin die Verzweiflung mich antreibt.
Denn mein Vater, er hat die entscheidenden Worte gesprochen,
Und sein Haus ist nicht mehr das meine, wenn er das Mädchen
Ausschließt, das ich allein nach Haus zu führen begehre.

Da versetzte behend die gute verständige Mutter:
Stehen wie Felsen doch zwei Männer gegeneinander!
Unbewegt und stolz will keiner dem andern sich nähern,
Keiner zum guten Worte, dem ersten, die Zunge bewegen.
Darum sag ich dir, Sohn: noch lebt die Hoffnung in meinem
Herzen, daß er sie dir, wenn sie gut und brav ist, verlobe,
Obgleich arm, so entschieden er auch die Arme versagt hat.
Denn er redet gar manches in seiner heftigen Art aus,
Das er doch nicht vollbringt; so gibt er auch zu das Versagte.
Aber ein gutes Wort verlangt er, und kann es verlangen;
Denn er ist Vater! Auch wissen wir wohl, sein Zorn ist nach Tische,
Wo er heftiger spricht und anderer Gründe bezweifelt,
Nie bedeutend; es reget der Wein dann jegliche Kraft auf
Seines heftigen Wollens, und läßt ihn die Worte der andern
Nicht vernehmen, er hört und fühlt alleine sich selber.
Aber es kommt der Abend heran, und die vielen Gespräche
Sind nun zwischen ihm und seinen Freunden gewechselt.

For I can sense that love, when it fastens its own bonds, releases
Every other commitment; and not the woman alone leaves 220
Father and mother behind when she follows the man she has chosen;
Also the man will remember his filial duties no longer,
If he perceives that his darling, his only belovèd, is going.
Therefore, permit me to do what my desperate spirit commands me;
For my father has said to me things that have forced this decision,
And I no longer consider his house to be mine; if he shuts his
Door to that woman, of all in the country, whom I want to marry."

Then with dexterous words his intelligent mother responded:
"Two men stand, I can see, like rocks opposing each other.
Neither approaches the other, so proud and so obstinate are they. 230
Neither will stir up his tongue to utter the first word of kindness.
Therefore I tell you, my son, of the hope still alive in my heart that
He will permit your betrothal, if she is as good as you tell us,
Penniless though she may be, and despite his former refusal.
For he often declares in his violent manner intentions
Which he can never make good on, and later retracts his refusal.
But he requires a courteous word, and rightly requires it,
For the man is your father. And also we know for a fact that
After a heavy repast, when he speaks with impetuous wrath and
Contradicts others' opinions, his anger signifies little. 240
Wine then inflames all the vigorous force of his will and he cannot
Hear what the others are saying; he feels and he hears but his own voice.
But when the evening has come, his conversation is finished,
And he sits down with his friends and relaxes after his supper.

Milder ist er fürwahr, ich weiß, wenn das Räuschchen vorbei ist,
Und er das Unrecht fühlt, das er andern lebhaft erzeigte.
Komm! wir wagen es gleich: das Frischgewagte gerät nur,
Und wir bedürfen der Freunde, die jetzo bei ihm noch versammelt
Sitzen; besonders wird uns der würdige Geistliche helfen.
Also sprach sie behende, und zog vom Steine sich hebend,
Auch vom Sitze den Sohn, den willig folgenden. Beide
Kamen schweigend herunter, den wichtigen Vorsatz bedenkend.

V

POLYHYMNIA

Der Weltbürger

Aber es saßen die drei noch immer sprechend zusammen,
Mit dem geistlichen Herrn der Apotheker beim Wirte,
Und es war das Gespräch noch immer ebendasselbe,
Das viel hin und her nach allen Seiten geführt ward.
Aber der treffliche Pfarrer versetzte, würdig gesinnt, drauf:
Widersprechen will ich euch nicht. Ich weiß es, der Mensch soll
Immer streben zum Bessern; und, wie wir sehen, er strebt auch
Immer dem Höheren nach, zum wenigsten sucht er das Neue.
Aber geht nicht zu weit! Denn neben diesen Gefühlen
Gab die Natur uns auch die Lust zu verharren im Alten,
Und sich dessen zu freun, was jeder lange gewohnt ist.
Aller Zustand ist gut, der natürlich ist und vernünftig.
Vieles wünscht sich der Mensch, und doch bedarf er nur wenig;

Gentler he is, I assure you, as soon as his wineglass is empty,
And he can sense the injustice his words have inflicted on others.
Come, let us try it at once; for nothing is gained unless ventured.
We are in need of the friends who still are assembled there
with him;
Most of all, to be sure, the reverend pastor will help us."
Thus she spoke, with decision, and rose from where she was sitting, 250
Helping also her son to rise, and he willingly followed.
Silently then they descended, and pondered their grave
undertaking.

V

POLYHYMNIA

The Citizen of the World

But the men, all three of them, still were conversing together,
Druggist, and pastor, and innkeeper, talking like bosom
companions.
So they continued to speak discussing still the same topic,
Turning it this way and that way, digressing in every direction.
But the reverend pastor, with worthy intention, responded:
"I would not contradict you. For man must be ever in
search of
That which is better; and, as we see him, he also endeavors
Ever to reach what is higher; at least he seeks for
renewal.
But you must not go too far! Besides these deeper emotions
Nature has given us also the joy of adhering to old ways, 10
And of rejoicing in that which has long been dear and familiar.
Every condition is good which conforms to Nature and Reason.
Great is the yearning of man; his necessities simple
and modest;

Denn die Tage sind kurz, und beschränkt der Sterblichen Schicksal.
Niemals tadl' ich den Mann, der immer, tätig und rastlos
Umgetrieben, das Meer und alle Straßen der Erde
Kühn und emsig befährt und sich des Gewinnes erfreuet,
Welcher sich reichlich um ihn und um die Seinen herum häuft;
Aber jener ist auch mir wert, der ruhige Bürger,
Der sein väterlich Erbe mit stillen Schritten umgehet,
Und die Erde besorgt, so wie es die Stunden gebieten.
Nicht verändert sich ihm in jedem Jahre der Boden,
Nicht streckt eilig der Baum, der neugepflanzte, die Arme
Gegen den Himmel aus, mit reichlichen Blüten gezieret.
Nein, der Mann bedarf der Geduld, er bedarf auch des reinen,
Immer gleichen, ruhigen Sinns und des graden Verstandes.
Denn nur wenige Samen vertraut er der nährenden Erde,
Wenige Tiere nur versteht er, mehrend, zu ziehen;
Denn das Nützliche bleibt allein sein ganzer Gedanke.
Glücklich, wem die Natur ein so gestimmtes Gemüt gab!
Er ernähret uns alle. Und Heil dem Bürger des kleinen
Städtchens, welcher ländlich Gewerb mit Bürgergewerb paart!
Auf ihm liegt nicht der Druck, der ängstlich den Landmann beschränket;
Ihn verwirrt nicht die Sorge der vielbegehrenden Städter,
Die dem Reicheren stets und dem Höheren, wenig vermögend,
Nachzustreben gewohnt sind, besonders die Weiber und Mädchen.
Segnet immer darum des Sohnes ruhig Bemühen,
Und die Gattin, die einst er, die gleichgesinnte, sich wählet.

Also sprach er. Es trat die Mutter zugleich mit dem Sohn ein,
Führend ihn bei der Hand und vor den Gatten ihn stellend.
Vater, sprach sie, wie oft gedachten wir, untereinander

For his days are but brief, and fate sets limits for mortals.
Never is he to be censured, who, constantly active and restless,
Driven about, traverses the seas and roads of the earth with
Boldness and industry, glad in his prosperous plentiful harvest,
Which he keeps piling about him, and storing up for his children.
But I value the citizen also, who quietly, calmly
Walks with unperturbed steps around his inherited land, and 20
Tills the earth in its season, as time and necessity order.
Nor does the soil, with every new year, present change to
its owner;
And the new planted tree does not hurry its growth as it lifts its
Branches, adorned with numberless blossoms, up to the heavens.
No, what is needed is patience; a man is likewise in need of
Character, pure and consistent, of candid intelligent goodness.
For but few are the seeds he entrusts to the nourishing earth, and
Few are the beasts he can raise with a hope to increase them
in number,
For the useful alone prevails as his focus of thinking.
Happy is he who by nature possesses a firm disposition. 30
He provides food for us all. And hail to the townsmen who live in
Cities of moderate size, who can couple farming with business.
There is no pressure on them such as that which inhibits
the rustic;
Nor are they troubled by worry, like those who inhabit the cities,
Eager to emulate wealthier people, to strive for advancement.
This is a weakness especially found in the women and maidens.
Bless therefore always the quiet endeavor of Hermann, and
welcome
Into your family the likeminded girl he some day will marry."

Thus he spoke, and that moment the mother and son, whom
she held by
His hand, entered the room; she brought him in front of his 40
father.
"Father," she said, "how often, in intimate chats with each other,

Schwatzend, des fröhlichen Tags, der kommen würde, wenn künftig
Hermann, seine Braut sich erwählend, uns endlich erfreute!
Hin und wider dachten wir da; bald dieses, bald jenes
Mädchen bestimmten wir ihm mit elterlichem Geschwätze
Nun ist er kommen der Tag; nun hat die Braut ihm der Himmel
Hergeführt und gezeigt, es hat sein Herz nun entschieden.
Sagten wir damals nicht immer: er solle selber sich wählen?
Wünschtest du nicht noch vorhin, er möchte heiter und lebhaft
Für ein Mädchen empfinden? Nun ist die Stunde gekommen!
Ja, er hat gefühlt und gewählt, und ist männlich entschieden.
Jenes Mädchen ist's, die Fremde, die ihm begegnet.
Gib sie ihm; oder er bleibt, so schwur er, im ledigen Stande.

Und es sagte der Sohn: Die gebt mir, Vater! Mein Herz hat
Rein und sicher gewählt; euch ist sie die würdigste Tochter.

Aber der Vater schwieg. Da stand der Geistliche schnell auf,
Nahm das Wort und sprach: Der Augenblick nur entscheidet
Über das Leben des Menschen und über sein ganzes Geschicke;
Denn nach langer Beratung ist doch ein jeder Entschluß nur
Werk des Moments, es ergreift doch nur der Verständge das Rechte.
Immer gefährlicher ist's, beim Wählen dieses und jenes
Nebenher zu bedenken und so das Gefühl zu verwirren.
Rein ist Hermann; ich kenn ihn von Jugend auf; und er streckte
Schon als Knabe die Hände nicht aus nach diesem und jenem.

Have we envisaged the radiant day of the future, when Hermann,
Choosing a bride for himself, would gladden the heart of
his parents?
Back and forth went our thoughts; now this girl, now that one
appeared to
Us to be best, in parental discussion, and so we decided.
Now the day has arrived, for heaven has brought him a bride,
and finally
Shown her to him, and his heart has finally made its decision.
Were we not always agreed that he should be free in his choosing?
Did you not wish just before that some girl would arouse and
inspire him?
Now the glad hour is here, when his heart and his mind are
at one, and 50
He has taken a man's resolution, and chosen the maiden
Whom he spoke of before, whom he met with the wandering
exiles.
Give her to him; else he swears he will stay as a bachelor forever."

Hermann then pled with his father: "O give me the maiden!
My heart has
Chosen in goodness and truth. And to you she will be a
good daughter."

But his father was silent. Then quickly the pastor arose and
Spoke with authority: "All in a moment the life of a man is
Settled forever; his destiny fixed and determined, forever.
Every decision is only the work of a moment, in spite of
Long consultation, and only intelligent men can be sure of 60
Taking the right resolution. And danger increases, in choosing,
If, by the way, this or that is considered, and feelings are puzzled.
Hermann is *good:* I have known him since earliest childhood,
and never,
When he was young, would he reach for a goal with a
lack of discernment.

Was er begehrte, das war ihm gemäß; so hielt er es fest auch.
Seid nicht scheu und verwundert, daß nun auf einmal erscheinet,
Was ihr so lange gewünscht. Es hat die Erscheinung fürwahr nicht
Jetzt die Gestalt des Wunsches, so wie ihr ihn etwa geheget.
Denn die Wünsche verhüllen uns selbst das Gewünschte; die Gaben
Kommen von oben herab, in ihren eignen Gestalten.
Nun verkennet es nicht, das Mädchen, das eurem geliebten,
Guten, verständigen Sohn zuerst die Seele bewegt hat.
Glücklich ist der, dem sogleich die erste Geliebte die Hand reicht,
Dem der lieblichste Wunsch nicht heimlich im Herzen verschmachtet!
Ja, ich seh es ihm an, es ist sein Schicksal entschieden.
Wahre Neigung vollendet sogleich zum Manne den Jüngling.
Nicht beweglich ist er; ich fürchte, versagt ihr ihm dieses,
Gehen die Jahre dahin, die schönsten, in traurigem Leben.

Da versetzte sogleich der Apotheker bedächtig,
Dem schon lange das Wort von der Lippe zu springen bereit war:
Laßt uns auch diesmal doch nur die Mittelstraße betreten!
Eile mit Weile! das war selbst Kaiser Augustus' Devise.
Gerne schick ich mich an, den lieben Nachbarn zu dienen,
Meinen geringen Verstand zu ihrem Nutzen zu brauchen:
Und besonders bedarf die Jugend, daß man sie leite.
Laßt mich also hinaus; ich will es prüfen, das Mädchen,
Will die Gemeinde befragen, in der sie lebt und bekannt ist.
Niemand betrügt mich so leicht; ich weiß die Worte zu schätzen.

Da versetzte sogleich der Sohn mit geflügelten Worten:

What he desired was befitting, and what he acquired he would cherish.
Be not surprised nor embarrassed that now a sudden fulfillment
Of your most cherished wish has arrived; to be sure its appearance
Does not agree with exactness with what you have always imagined.
Wishes obscure their objective; fulfillment is not as expected.
That which is given comes down from above, in a form which is proper. 70
Do not misjudge the girl who was first to enkindle the spirit
Of your cherished intelligent son: no other could do it.
Happy is he who succeeds in winning the first girl he chooses,
So that his dearest of wishes can never be buried within him.
Yes, I can see it quite clearly—his fate is decided forever.
True inclination can ripen a youth to a man in a moment.
Nor is he fickle; I fear that, if you refuse him permission,
Life's most beautiful years will be passed in sadness and sorrow."

Quickly the druggist replied to his friend, expressing his caution;
Long had his lips been desirous of launching the fruit of his thinking: 80
"Let us remember, as always, to walk on the road in the middle.
'Hasten with caution' was chosen as motto by Caesar Augustus.
I declare myself ready to do my neighbors a service,
Ready to use my modest intelligence so as to help them;
Youth is especially in need of the proper direction and guidance.
So permit me to leave you, and closely examine this maiden,
Ask the people who know her, and live with her always, about her.
I am not easily deceived, for I know how to judge what they tell me."

Then, with jubilant words, did Hermann respond to the neighbor:

Tut es, Nachbar, und geht und erkundigt euch. Aber ich wünsche,
Daß der Herr Pfarrer sich auch in eurer Gesellschaft befinde;
Zwei so treffliche Männer sind unverwerfliche Zeugen.
O, mein Vater! sie ist nicht hergelaufen, das Mädchen,
Keine, die durch das Land auf Abenteuer umherschweift,
Und den Jüngling bestrickt, den unerfahrnen, mit Ränken.
Nein; das wilde Geschick des allverderblichen Krieges,
Das die Welt zerstört und manches feste Gebäude
Schon aus dem Grunde gehoben, hat auch die Arme vertrieben.
Streifen nicht herrliche Männer von hoher Geburt nun im Elend?
Fürsten fliehen vermummt, und Könige leben verbannet.
Ach, so ist auch sie, von ihren Schwestern die beste,
Aus dem Lande getrieben; ihr eignes Unglück vergessend,
Steht sie anderen bei, ist ohne Hülfe noch hülfreich.
Groß sind Jammer und Not, die über die Erde sich breiten;
Sollte nicht auch ein Glück aus diesem Unglück hervorgehn,
Und ich, im Arme der Braut, der zuverlässigen Gattin,
Mich nicht erfreuen des Kriegs, so wie ihr des Brandes euch freutet?

Da versetzte der Vater, und tat bedeutend den Mund auf:
Wie ist, o Sohn, dir die Zunge gelöst, die schon dir im Munde
Lange Jahre gestockt, und nur sich dürftig bewegte!
Muß ich doch heut erfahren, was jedem Vater gedroht ist:
Daß den Willen des Sohns, den heftigen, gerne die Mutter
Allzugelind begünstigt, und jeder Nachbar Partei nimmt,
Wenn es über den Vater nur hergeht oder den Ehmann.
Aber ich will euch zusammen nicht widerstehen; was hülf es?
Denn ich sehe doch schon hier Trotz und Tränen im voraus.
Gehet und prüfet, und bringt in Gottes Namen die Tochter

"Do so, dear neighbor, I beg you! Go and inquire, but I wish that 90
You would associate with you his reverence our pastor, for counsel.
Two such excellent men will provide unimpeachable witness.
Father, the girl is no vagrant, roaming in search of adventure
Over the countryside, seeking an innocent lad to entrap with
Cunning and vicious intention of causing his downfall and ruin.
No, the terrible fate of this murderous war, which has shattered
All of the world, and has torn from its footing even the firmest
Building, has driven also this girl from her home into exile.
Are not magnificent men of the noblest of families in hardship?
Princes are fleeing disguised, and the kings, their fathers, 100
are banished.
Yes, she, the best of her sisters, is also displaced from her country;
Mindful of others alone, and forgetful of personal suffering,
She is a solace to all, in despite of her own dire misfortune.
Great is the trouble and wretchedness spreading all over these
countries:
Could there not spring from this sorrow some joy? Could not
I, in the arms of
My bride, trusted companion and wife, rejoice in the war, as
You long ago once also rejoiced in a great conflagration?"

Then did his father reply, giving voice with meaningful vigor:
"How does it happen, my son, that your tongue has been
suddenly loosened,
Which for long years has stuck in your mouth and moved 110
only seldom?
I have suffered today the destiny threatening all fathers:
That a mother with mildness will side with her violent son, and
Every neighbor will rally to bolster their common defense, if
Only their mutual aim be defeat of the father and husband.
But I will not resist your alliance—what good would it do me?
For I predict in advance the menacing tears and defiance.
Go, then, investigate; bring home a daughter, that all may be
peaceful;

Mir ins Haus; wo nicht, so mag er das Mädchen vergessen.

Also der Vater. Es rief der Sohn mit froher Gebärde:
Noch vor Abend ist euch die trefflichste Tochter bescheret,
Wie sie der Mann sich wünscht, dem ein kluger Sinn in der Brust lebt.
Glücklich ist die Gute dann auch, so darf ich es hoffen.
Ja, sie danket mir ewig, daß ich ihr Vater und Mutter
Wiedergegeben in euch, so wie sie verständige Kinder
Wünschen. Aber ich zaudre nicht mehr; ich schirre die Pferde
Gleich, und führe die Freunde hinaus auf die Spur der Geliebten,
Überlasse die Männer sich selbst und der eigenen Klugheit,
Richte, so schwör ich euch zu, mich ganz nach ihrer Entscheidung,
Und ich seh es nicht wieder, als bis es mein ist, das Mädchen.
Und so ging er hinaus, indessen manches die andern
Weislich erwogen und schnell die wichtige Sache besprachen.

Hermann eilte zum Stalle sogleich, wo die mutigen Hengste
Ruhig standen und rasch den reinen Hafer verzehrten,
Und das trockene Heu, auf der besten Wiese gehauen.
Eilig legt' er ihnen darauf das blanke Gebiß an,
Zog die Riemen sogleich durch die schön versilberten Schnallen,
Und befestigte dann die langen, breiteren Zügel,
Führte die Pferde heraus in den Hof, wo der willige Knecht schon
Vorgeschoben die Kutsche, sie leicht an der Deichsel bewegend.
Abgemessen knüpften sie drauf an die Waage mit saubern
Stricken die rasche Kraft der leicht hinziehenden Pferde.

If your decision be negative, let him forget her forever."

Thus spoke the father, and Hermann exclaimed with joyous expression:
"Even before tonight you will have an excellent daughter, 120
Such as a man would desire, whose judgment is sound and reflective.
Happy, I'm sure, she also will be, and I hope for her gladness.
Yes, she will thank me forever that I have given her parents
Like you, such as intelligent children would find most appealing.
But I must tarry no longer! At once I will harness the horses,
And I will drive our friends on the road in search of my darling,
Leaving the men to themselves, so as freely to use their best judgment.
I, for my part, I swear it, will always respect their decision,
Nor will I see her again until I can claim her acceptance."
Speaking thus he went out, while the others wisely considered 130
How they should handle the matter, and discussed this affair of importance.

Hermann hurried at once to the stable; the spirited stallions
Stood there at ease, consuming the clean and nourishing oats, and
Hay which was mown on the best of the meadows, and dried to perfection.
Quickly he fitted the gleaming bits in their mouths, then at once he
Pulled the straps through the buckles, beautifully silvered and polished;
Then he attached to the buckles the reins, which were longer and broader;
Led out the horses into the courtyard; the stable boy, willing,
Thither had brought him the coach, which to push by the shafts was quite easy.
Carefully then they attached to the whiffletree, tightly, with neatest 140
Cords, the swiftness and strength of the gracefully galloping horses.

Hermann faßte die Peitsche; dann saß er und rollt' in den
Torweg.
Als die Freunde nun gleich die geräumigen Plätze genommen,
Rollte der Wagen eilig, und ließ das Pflaster zurücke,
Ließ zurück die Mauern der Stadt und die reinlichen Türme.
So fuhr Hermann dahin, der wohlbekannten Chaussee zu,
Rasch, und säumete nicht und fuhr bergan wie bergunter.
Als er aber nunmehr den Turm des Dorfes erblickte,
Und nicht fern mehr lagen die gartenumgebenen Häuser,
Dacht er bei sich selbst, nun anzuhalten die Pferde.

Von dem würdigen Dunkel erhabener Linden umschattet,
Die Jahrhunderte schon an dieser Stelle gewurzelt,
War mit Rasen bedeckt ein weiter grünender Anger
Vor dem Dorfe, den Bauern und nahen Städtern ein Lustort.
Flachgegraben befand sich unter den Bäumen ein Brunnen.
Stieg man die Stufen hinab, so zeigten sich steinerne Bänke,
Rings um die Quelle gesetzt, die immer lebendig hervorquoll,
Reinlich, mit niedriger Mauer gefaßt, zu schöpfen
bequemlich.
Hermann aber beschloß, in diesem Schatten die Pferde
Mit dem Wagen zu halten. Er tat so, und sagte die Worte:
Steiget, Freunde, nun aus und geht, damit ihr erfahret,
Ob das Mädchen auch wert der Hand sei, die ich ihr biete.
Zwar ich glaub es, und mir erzählt ihr nichts Neues und
Seltnes;
Hätt ich allein zu tun, so ging ich behend zu dem Dorf hin,
Und mit wenigen Worten entschiede die Gute mein
Schicksal.
Und ihr werdet sie bald vor allen andern erkennen;
Denn wohl schwerlich ist an Bildung ihr eine vergleichbar.

Hermann, taking the whip, sat down, and the carriage rolled
forward
Into the gateway; the friends settled down in the comfortable
seats and
Swiftly the carriage rolled onward, leaving behind it the paving,
Leaving behind it the walls of the town with its profile of towers.
Thus then did Hermann drive on, directing the coach toward
the highway
Quickly, without hesitation, regardless of hills or of valleys.
But when at last he caught sight of the towering spire of the village,
And of its houses and gardens, no longer appearing so distant,
Then he thought to himself it was time to check his swift coursers. 150

There in front of the village, covered with grass and surrounded
By some venerable lindens, planted there centuries earlier,
Was a meadow, capacious and verdant, a place of refreshment
Meant for the farmers as well as the townsfolk whose homes
were not distant.
Under the trees was a spring, leveled shallowly off like a basin.
If one descended its steps, one encountered the benches of
stonework
Which had been placed round about the fountain eternally flowing,
Easy to draw from and clean, enclosed behind a low railing.
Hermann however selected this spot as a rest for his horses.
Here then he halted the carriage and said to the friends who 160
were with him:
"Now, please, get out of the carriage, my friends, and begin
your inquiry
Whether the girl is deserving or not of the marriage I offer.
I to be sure am convinced; you can bring me no news or surprises.
If I could do it myself I would go at once to the village,
And, with no loss of words, determine my fate from the maiden.
Now: you will easily tell her apart from all other women,
For I very much doubt whether any of them can be like her.

Aber ich geb euch noch die Zeichen der reinlichen Kleider:
Denn der rote Latz erhebt den gewölbeten Busen,
Schön geschnürt, und es liegt das schwarze Mieder ihr knapp an;
Sauber hat sie den Saum des Hemdes zur Krause gefaltet,
Die ihr das Kinn umgibt, das runde, mit reinlicher Anmut;
Frei und heiter zeigt sich des Kopfes zierliches Eirund;
Stark sind vielmal die Zöpfe um silberne Nadeln gewickelt;
Vielgefaltet und blau fängt unter dem Latze der Rock an
Und umschlägt ihr im Gehn die wohlgebildeten Knöchel.
Doch das will ich euch sagen, und noch mir ausdrücklich erbitten:
Redet nicht mit dem Mädchen, und laßt nicht merken die Absicht,
Sondern befraget die andern, und hört, was sie alles erzählen.
Habt ihr Nachricht genug, zu beruhigen Vater und Mutter,
Kehret zu mir dann zurück, und wir bedenken das Weitre.
Also dacht ich mir's aus, den Weg her, den wir gefahren.

Also sprach er. Es gingen darauf die Freunde dem Dorf zu.
Wo in Gärten und Scheunen und Häusern die Menge von Menschen
Wimmelte, Karrn an Karrn die breite Straße dahin stand.
Männer versorgten das brüllende Vieh und die Pferd an den Wagen,
Wäsche trockneten emsig auf allen Hecken die Weiber,
Und es ergötzten die Kinder sich plätschernd im Wasser des Baches.
Also durch die Wagen sich drängend, durch Menschen und Tiere,
Sahen sie rechts und links sich um, die gesendeten Späher,
Ob sie nicht etwa das Bild des bezeichneten Mädchens erblickten;
Aber keine von allen erschien die herrliche Jungfrau.
Stärker fanden sie bald das Gedränge. Da war um die Wagen

Let me explain to you how she is dressed, for her clothing
is spotless:
First a scarf of bright scarlet supports the curve of her bosom,
Beautifully laced and tied; and her bodice, all black, fits her snugly; 170
Neatly the hem of her blouse she has folded into a ruffle,
Framing her chin in its roundness with startling precision
and contrast.
Freely her motions display that her head is a delicate oval;
Silver hairpins serve as support for the weight of her tresses;
Under her scarf is her skirt, so blue and pleated so neatly
Reaching down to her beautiful ankles and swirling about her.
But there is one thing to tell you: I now must explicitly ask you:
Do not speak with the girl nor permit her to guess your intention,
But keep asking the others, and listen with care to their answers.
When you have found out enough to pacify father and mother, 180
Please return to me here, and we will take counsel together.
This is the way that I planned it as I was driving you hither."

Thus did he speak; thereafter his friends made their way to
the village,
Where in gardens and stables and houses the throngs of the exiles
Swarmed, and cart after cart was standing there on the roadway.
Men were tending the bellowing kine, and caring for horses;
Women were busily spreading their laundry to dry on the hedges.
And all the children were splashing and shouting with joy in
the water.
So as they passed through the crowd of the wagons, the beasts
and the people,
Looking to right and to left, the searchers continued their seeking. 190
Hoping to see and to know the girl by Hermann's
description;
But not a one of the many they saw resembled the maiden.
Soon the crowd became thicker. There in the press of the wagons

Streit der drohenden Männer, worein sich mischten die Weiber,
Schreiend. Da nahte sich schnell mit würdigen Schritten ein Alter,
Trat zu den Scheltenden hin; und sogleich verklang das Getöse,
Als er Ruhe gebot, und väterlich ernst sie bedrohte.
Hat uns, rief er, noch nicht das Unglück also gebändigt,
Daß wir endlich verstehn, uns untereinander zu dulden
Und zu vertragen, wenn auch nicht jeder die Handlungen abmißt?
Unverträglich fürwahr ist der Glückliche! Werden die Leiden
Endlich euch lehren, nicht mehr, wie sonst, mit dem Bruder zu hadern?
Gönnet einander den Platz auf fremdem Boden, und teilet
Was ihr habet, zusammen, damit ihr Barmherzigkeit findet.

Also sagte der Mann, und alle schwiegen; verträglich
Ordneten Vieh und Wagen die wieder besänftigten Menschen.
Als der Geistliche nun die Rede des Mannes vernommen,
Und den ruhigen Sinn des fremden Richters entdeckte,
Trat er an ihn heran, und sprach die bedeutenden Worte:
Vater, fürwahr! wenn das Volk in glücklichen Tagen dahin lebt,
Von der Erde sich nährend, die weit und breit sich auftut
Und die erwünschten Gaben in Jahren und Monden erneuert,
Da geht alles von selbst, und jeder ist sich der Klügste,
Wie der Beste; und so bestehen sie nebeneinander,
Und der vernünftigste Mann ist wie ein andrer gehalten:
Denn was alles geschieht, geht still, wie von selber, den Gang fort.
Aber zerrüttet die Not die gewöhnlichen Wege des Lebens,
Reißt das Gebäude nieder, und wühlet Garten und Saat um,
Treibt den Mann und das Weib vom Raume der traulichen Wohnung,

Angry men were exchanging threatening words, and the women
Mingled their screaming. Then quickly approached an elderly person
Who with great dignity stepped toward the quarrelers. At once
there was silence,
When, with fatherly fervor, he bade them be still and reproved them.
"Have we," he cried, "not yet been chastened enough by misfortune
That we can finally agree to put up with each other and bear it,
Even though not every one of us carefully considers his actions. 200
Selfish indeed are the fortunate. Has not our suffering taught you
Never to quarrel any more, as you used to do, with your brethren?
Give to each other some room, in this country of strangers; and justly
Share your possessions, that you may find adequate mercy from
others."

Such were the words of the man, and none raised objection;
in concord
Cattle and wagons were put into order by men in good temper.
When now the pastor had heard what the man had done by
his counsel,
And had discovered how balanced and calm was this judge of
the exiles,
He stepped up to him boldly and spoke to him words of
of importance.
"Father, in truth, when a people lives on in days of good fortune, 210
Drawing their food from the earth, which opens its treasures
before them,
And by month and by year keeps renewing its generous harvest,
Everything goes by itself, and every man seems to himself the
Wisest and best, and people can live in concord together,
Even the wisest of men is considered to be like the others,
For, whatever may happen, life runs its course without turmoil.
But if trouble destroys the accustomed manner of living,
Tears down the houses, and roots up the well planted gardens
of harvest,
Drives the man with his wife from the shelter of intimate living,

Schleppt in die Irre sie fort, durch ängstliche Tage und Nächte:
Ach! da sieht man sich um, wer wohl der verständigste Mann sei,
Und er redet nicht mehr die herrlichen Worte vergebens.
Sagt mir, Vater, ihr seid gewiß der Richter von diesen
Flüchtigen Männern, der ihr sogleich die Gemüter beruhigt?
Ja, ihr erscheint mir heut als einer der ältesten Führer,
Die durch Wüsten und Irren vertriebene Völker geleitet.
Denk ich doch eben, ich rede mit Josua oder mit Moses.

Und es versetzte darauf mit ernstem Blicke der Richter:
Wahrlich unsere Zeit vergleicht sich den seltensten Zeiten,
Die die Geschichte bemerkt, die heilige wie die gemeine.
Denn wer gestern und heut in diesen Tagen gelebt hat,
Hat schon Jahre gelebt: so drängen sich alle Geschichten.
Denk ich ein wenig zurück, so scheint mir ein graues Alter
Auf dem Haupte zu liegen, und doch ist die Kraft noch lebendig.
O, wir anderen dürfen uns wohl mit jenen vergleichen,
Denen in ernster Stund erschien im feurigen Busche
Gott der Herr; auch uns erschien er in Wolken und Feuer.

Als nun der Pfarrer darauf noch weiter zu sprechen geneigt war
Und das Schicksal des Manns und der Seinen zu hören verlangte,
Sagte behend der Gefährte mit heimlichen Worten ins Ohr ihm:
Sprecht mit dem Richter nur fort, und bringt das Gespräch auf das Mädchen.
Aber ich gehe herum, sie aufzusuchen, und komme
Wieder, sobald ich sie finde. Es nickte der Pfarrer dagegen,
Und durch die Hecken und Gärten und Scheunen suchte der Späher.

Drags them forth into exile, through days and night full of terror, 220
Ah, then one searches about to find an intelligent leader,
And no longer he speaks his glorious words unavailing.
Tell me, good father, you are, I presume, the judge of those exiles,
Whose intemperate spirits your words have calmed and corrected?
Yes, you appear to be one of the Biblical leaders,
Who in their banishment led the wandering hosts through the deserts,
And I imagine I'm speaking with Joshua, even with Moses."

Then, with a serious mien, the judge replied to the pastor:
"Truly our times do resemble the rarest of times of the ancients,
Which our history records, the sacred as well as the worldly. 230
For whoever has lived but today and yesterday only
Lately has lived through years; so that stories keep crowding each other.
If I think back just a little, it seems that my years are unnumbered,
Yet my strength is alive, and my vigor is still unabated.
O, we moderns indeed may liken ourselves to those others,
Who in a serious hour beheld in a bush all a-flaming
God the Lord; to us, too, He appeared in the clouds and in wildfire."

When now the pastor was starting to speak with the judge even further,
Seeking to learn what he could of the fate of the man and his family,
Quickly into his ear his partner furtively whispered: 240
"Please continue to speak with the judge, and mention the maiden!
I however will look all about and find where she is, and
Swiftly return, the moment I find her." The pastor assented,
And, through gardens and hedges and stables the searcher then sought her.

VI

KLIO

Das Zeitalter

Als nun der geistliche Herr den fremden Richter befragte,
Was die Gemeine gelitten, wie lang sie von Hause vertrieben;
Sagte der Mann darauf: Nicht kurz sind unsere Leiden;
Denn wir haben das Bittre der sämtlichen Jahre getrunken,
Schrecklicher, weil auch uns die schönste Hoffnung zerstört ward.
Denn wer leugnet es wohl, daß hoch sich das Herz ihm erhoben,
Ihm die freiere Brust mit reineren Pulsen geschlagen,
Als sich der erste Glanz der neuen Sonne heranhob,
Als man hörte vom Rechte der Menschen, das allen gemein sei,
Von der begeisternden Freiheit und von der löblichen Gleichheit!
Damals hoffte jeder sich selbst zu leben; es schien sich
Aufzulösen das Band, das viele Länder umstrickte,
Das der Müßiggang und der Eigennutz in der Hand hielt.
Schauten nicht alle Völker in jenen drängenden Tagen
Nach der Hauptstadt der Welt, die es schon so lange gewesen,
Und jetzt mehr als je den herrlichen Namen verdiente?
Waren nicht jener Männer, der ersten Verkünder der Botschaft,
Namen den höchsten gleich, die unter die Sterne gesetzt sind?
Wuchs nicht jeglichem Menschen der Mut und der Geist und die Sprache?

VI

CLIO

The Times

When now the reverend pastor inquired of the judge of
the exiles
What his people had suffered and how long their banishment lasted,
Then he received the reply: "Too long has our misery lasted!
For we have swallowed the bitterness which through the years
has engulfed us,
Even more terribly, in that our fairest of hopes has been shattered.
For who could ever deny that his heart was perceptibly lifted,
Or that his pulses beat faster, and his chest was expanded
in freedom,
When the first dawn of the new sun's brilliance rose in the
heavens,
When we heard of the rights of mankind, which are common to
all men,
Heard of freedom, inspiring to all, and that all men are equal, 10
Then hope stirred in us all of living according to nature;
Then it seemed that the bonds which constricted the nations
were loosened,
Bonds which were held in the hands of those who were selfish
and idle.
Did not the nations look in those days of oppression and rancor
Toward the notable capital of the whole world, which had always
Been considered as such, and deserved it now more than ever?
Did not the names of the men who were first to proclaim the
new message
Rank with the highest of names which are worshipped as stars
in the heavens?
Was there not increase in all of courage, of speech, and of spirit?

Und wir waren zuerst, als Nachbarn, lebhaft entzündet.
Drauf begann der Krieg, und die Züge bewaffneter Franken
Rückten näher; allein sie schienen nur Freundschaft zu bringen.
Und die brachten sie auch: denn ihnen erhöht war die Seele
Allen; sie pflanzten mit Lust die munteren Bäume der Freiheit,
Jedem das Seine versprechend, und jedem die eigne Regierung;
Hoch erfreute sich da die Jugend, sich freute das Alter,
Und der muntere Tanz begann um die neue Standarte.
So gewannen sie bald, die überwiegenden Franken,
Erst der Männer Geist, mit feurigem munterm Beginnen,
Dann die Herzen der Weiber, mit unwiderstehlicher Anmut.
Leicht selbst schien uns der Druck des vielbedürfenden Krieges;
Denn die Hoffnung umschwebte vor unsern Augen die Ferne,
Lockte die Blicke hinaus in neueröffnete Bahnen.

O, wie froh ist die Zeit, wenn mit der Braut sich der Bräutgam
Schwinget im Tanze, den Tag der gewünschten Verbindung erwartend!
Aber herrlicher war die Zeit, in der uns das Höchste,
Was der Mensch sich denkt, als nah und erreichbar gezeigt ward.
Da war jedem die Zunge gelöst; es sprachen die Greise,
Männer und Jünglinge laut voll hohen Sinns und Gefühles.

Aber der Himmel trübte sich bald. Um den Vorteil der Herrschaft
Stritt ein verderbtes Geschlecht, unwürdig das Gute zu schaffen.
Sie ermordeten sich und unterdrückten die neuen

And, at first, as their neighbors, we felt that a spark had been kindled. 20
Then came the start of the war, and the armed troops of the Frenchmen
Moved ever closer: but still they seemed to bring friendship, not hatred.
Friendship indeed they did bring: and every man's soul was exalted;
Gladly they planted the cheerful liberty trees and adorned them,
Pledging to each one his own and a government formed by his choosing.
Great was the joy of the young, and the old people shared in their gladness;
Thus around the new banner began the cheerful rejoicing.
So the dominant Frenchmen soon took control of the spirits
And of the minds of the men, at first, with their challenging doings;
Then the hearts of the women succumbed to their charm, unresisting. 30
Even the pressure of war was quite insufficient to faze us;
For in the distance we saw the soaring figure of hope, which
Lured our longing away to pathways newly discovered.

O how happy the time when a couple betrothèd are dancing,
Waiting with joy and with hope for the day that will join them together!
Even more glad was the time when the highest of dreams and ambitions
Ever conceived of by man were seen to be ready for grasping;
Then did everyone utter his thoughts: both the old and the young men
Spoke with conviction and ardor, full of emotion and purpose.

Soon however the sky became clouded. The summit of power 40
Now was sought by a bad generation, unable, unworthy
Ever of doing the good. They murdered each other, suppressing

Nachbarn und Brüder, und sandten die eigennützige Menge.
Und es praßten bei uns die Obern, und raubten im großen,
Und es raubten und praßten bis zu dem Kleinsten die Kleinen;
Jeder schien nur besorgt, es bleibe was übrig für morgen.
Allzugroß war die Not, und täglich wuchs die Bedrückung;
Niemand vernahm das Geschrei, sie waren die Herren des Tages.
Da fiel Kummer und Wut auch selbst ein gelaßnes Gemüt an;
Jeder sann nur und schwur, die Beleidigung alle zu rächen,
Und den bittern Verlust der doppelt betrogenen Hoffnung.
Und es wendete sich das Glück auf die Seite der Deutschen,
Und der Franke floh mit eiligen Märschen zurücke.
Ach, da fühlten wir erst das traurige Schicksal des Krieges!
Denn der Sieger ist groß und gut; zum wenigsten scheint er's
Und er schonet den Mann, den besiegten, als wär er der seine,
Wenn er ihm täglich nützt und mit den Gütern ihm dienet.
Aber der Flüchtige kennt kein Gesetz; denn er wehrt nur den Tod ab,
Und verzehret nur schnell und ohne Rücksicht die Güter.
Dann ist sein Gemüt auch erhitzt, und es kehrt die Verzweiflung
Aus dem Herzen hervor das frevelhafte Beginnen.
Nichts ist heilig ihm mehr; er raubt es. Die wilde Begierde
Dringt mit Gewalt auf das Weib, und macht die Lust zum Entsetzen.
Überall sieht er den Tod, und genießt die letzten Minuten
Grausam, freut sich des Bluts, und freut sich des heulenden Jammers.

Grimmig erhob sich darauf in unsern Männern die Wut nun,
Das Verlorne zu rächen und zu verteidgen die Reste.
Alles ergriff die Waffen, gelockt von der Eile des Flüchtlings,
Und vom blassen Gesicht und scheu unsicheren Blicke.

New friends, neighbors and brothers, electing their own greedy rabble.
Here among us our superiors revelled and robbed on a grand scale,
And the lesser ones revelled and robbed, right down to the smallest;
Everyone seemed quite afraid to have anything left for the morrow.
Dreadful was our distress, and oppression was daily increasing;
None would give heed to the outcry against them, for they were in power.
Even the calmest of minds was a-tremble with sorrow and anger;
Everyone plotted and swore to avenge this insulting behavior, 50
Also the bitter privation of hope, which had double deceived us.
Then the favor of fortune directed itself toward the Germans,
And in hasty retreat the Frenchmen returned to their country.
Only now did we feel war's sorrowful fate overwhelm us.
For the victor is great and good: at least he appears so,
And he is kind to the conquered, as if they were part of his people,
If they can daily be useful to him and their goods are of service.
But the fugitive knows not the law; for he seeks but to shun death
And, incautiously, quickly consumes his treasured possessions.
Then are his spirits enkindled, and from the despair of his heart his 60
Criminal enterprise takes its beginning. For nothing is holy—
All that he sees is his prey: and even an innocent woman
Falls as his victim; he rapes her and changes desire into horror.
Death is everywhere present before him; he gloats on the dying,
Savagely glad of the gore and the shrieks and wails of the victims.

Fiercely there grew in the hearts of our men a furious anger,
Aimed at avenging their losses, determined to save what was left them.
Everyone reached for his weapons, led on by the fugitives' hurry,
And by their pallor of face, and their furtive air of unsureness.

Rastlos nun erklang das Getön der stürmenden Glocke
Und die künftge Gefahr hielt nicht die grimmige Wut auf.
Schnell verwandelte sich des Feldbaus friedliche Rüstung
Nun in Wehre; da troff von Blute Gabel und Sense.
Ohne Begnadigung fiel der Feind, und ohne Verschonung;
Überall raste die Wut und die feige tückische Schwäche.
Möcht ich den Menschen doch nie in dieser schnöden Verirrung
Wiedersehn! Das wütende Tier ist ein besserer Anblick.
Sprech er doch nie von Freiheit, als könn er sich selber regieren!
Losgebunden erscheint, sobald die Schranken hinweg sind,
Alles Böse, das tief das Gesetz in die Winkel zurücktrieb.

Trefflicher Mann! versetzte darauf der Pfarrer mit Nachdruck:
Wenn ihr den Menschen verkennt, so kann ich euch darum nicht schelten;
Habt ihr doch Böses genug erlitten vom wüsten Beginnen!
Wolltet ihr aber zurück die traurigen Tage durchschauen,
Würdet ihr selber gestehen, wie oft ihr auch Gutes erblicktet,
Manches Treffliche, das verborgen bleibt in dem Herzen,
Regt die Gefahr es nicht auf, und drängt die Not nicht den Menschen,
Daß er als Engel sich zeig, erscheine den andern ein Schutzgott.

Lächelnd versetzte darauf der alte würdige Richter:
Ihr erinnert mich klug, wie oft nach dem Brande des Hauses
Man den betrübten Besitzer an Gold und Silber erinnert,
Das geschmolzen im Schutt nun überblieben zerstreut liegt.
Wenig ist es fürwahr, doch auch das wenige köstlich;
Und der Verarmte gräbet ihm nach, und freut sich des Fundes.

Now there rang out unceasing the sound of the clanging
alarm bell, 70
And the danger to come was unable to stem their fierce fury.
Quickly the tools of the farm and the field were transformed
into weapons:
Pitchfork and scythe were soon dripping with blood, of those
who had fallen.
And without mercy the foe was cut down, without any sparing.
Everywhere fury was rampant, and cowardly, treacherous weakness.
O, may I never be witness again to such baseness of conduct;
Animals, raging and savage, are better by far than such humans.
Let man never discuss independence, as thought he were ever
Able to govern himself! As soon as the barrier is lowered,
All the evil breaks loose which the law had curbed by its pressure." 80

"Excellent man!" the pastor responded to this, with approval:
"I cannot blame you if you are harsh with mankind in your
judgment.
Truly you suffered enough from all that disorderly conduct!
But, if you cast your thought back to the days of your sorrow
and trouble,
You would be forced to admit, inasmuch as you often observed
their
Kindness in action, that much of men's goodness stays locked in
their hearts till
Danger excites them, or till necessity forces the issue.
Then they show themselves angels, and appear like saviors
to others."

Then with a smile the elderly dignified magistrate answered:
"Wisely you show me, as often one shows the sorrowful owner 90
Of a house that has burned, that his gold and silver are present,
Scattered all through the ruins, but undiminished in value.
True, it is not very much, but even the little is precious,
And the impoverished man digs it up and is glad he has found it.

Und so kehr ich auch gern die heitern Gedanken zu jenen
Wenigen guten Taten, die aufbewahrt das Gedächtnis.
Ja, ich will es nicht leugnen, ich sah sich Feinde versöhnen,
Um die Stadt vom Übel zu retten; ich sah auch der Freunde,
Sah der Eltern Lieb und der Kinder Unmögliches wagen;
Sah wie der Jüngling auf einmal zum Mann ward: sah wie der Greis sich
Wieder verjüngte, das Kind sich selbst als Jüngling enthüllte.
Ja, und das schwache Geschlecht, so wie es gewöhnlich genannt wird,
Zeigte sich tapfer und mächtig, und gegenwärtigen Geistes.
Und so laßt mich vor allen der schönen Tat noch erwähnen,
Die hochherzig ein Mädchen vollbrachte, die treffliche Jungfrau,
Die auf dem großen Gehöft allein mit den Mädchen zurückblieb;
Denn es waren die Männer auch gegen die Fremden gezogen.
Da überfiel den Hof ein Trupp verlaufnen Gesindels,
Plündernd, und drängte sogleich sich in die Zimmer der Frauen.
Sie erblickten das Bild der schön erwachsenen Jungfrau
Und die lieblichen Mädchen, noch eher Kinder zu heißen.
Da ergriff sie wilde Begier; sie stürmten gefühllos
Auf die zitternde Schar und aufs hochherzige Mädchen.
Aber sie riß dem einen sogleich von der Seite den Säbel,
Hieb ihn nieder gewaltig; er stürzt' ihr blutend zu Füßen.
Dann mit männlichen Streichen befreite sie tapfer die Mädchen,
Traf noch viere der Räuber; doch die entflohen dem Tode.
Dann verschloß sie den Hof, und harrte der Hülfe, bewaffnet.

Thus I also am pleased, when I think, with cheerful
remememberance,
Of the handful of deeds which my memory records for their
goodness.
Yes, I will not deny it: I saw how enemies' hatred
All was forgotten, to save the city from evil, how friends and
Parents and children would take impossible risks for each other;
Youths of a sudden turned into men, and oldsters grew youthful;
Those who were babies revealed themselves now as strong
adolescents. 100
Yes, why even the weaker sex, as we call it, was brave and
Strong, and cool under pressure, stood firm in the direst disaster.
Now let me speak of the wonderful deed that was done by
a maiden,
Bravest and best of her sex, who remained at the farm with
the others,
When all the men had gone out to encounter the strangers and
fight them.
Suddenly, there at the farm, there appeared some undisciplined
villains,
Robbing and looting; at once they entered the rooms of
the women,
Where they caught sight of this beautiful girl as she stood
with the others, 110
Most of them young, as children might be, but surpassingly lovely.
Then they were seized by intemperate lust, and rushed
without mercy
Straight at the trembling young girls and their stalwart
valiant protectress.
But in a trice she snatched from the side of the one man his sabre,
Striking him violently down, and he fell bleeding before her.
Then with vigorous strokes she boldly slashed at the others,
Wounding four more, and freeing the girls. But the wounded
escaped. Then,
Sabre in hand, she bolted the gate and awaited assistance.

Als der Geistliche nun das Lob des Mädchen vernommen,
Stieg die Hoffnung sogleich für seinen Freund im Gemüt auf,
Und er war im Begriff zu fragen, wohin sie geraten?
Ob auf der traurigen Flucht sie nun mit dem Volk sich befinde?

Aber da trat herbei der Apotheker behende,
Zupfte den geistlichen Herrn, und sagte die wispernden Worte:
Hab ich doch endlich das Mädchen aus vielen hundert gefunden,
Nach der Beschreibung! So kommt und sehet sie selber mit Augen;
Nehmet den Richter mit euch, damit wir das Weitere hören.
Und sie kehrten sich um, und weg war gerufen der Richter
Von den Seinen, die ihn, bedürftig des Rates, verlangten.
Doch es folgte sogleich dem Apotheker der Pfarrherr
An die Lücke des Zauns, und jener deutete listig.
Seht ihr, sagt' er, das Mädchen? Sie hat die Puppe gewickelt,
Und ich erkenne genau den alten Kattun und den blauen
Kissenüberzug wohl, den ihr Hermann im Bündel gebracht hat.
Sie verwendete schnell, fürwahr, und gut die Geschenke.
Diese sind deutliche Zeichen, es treffen die übrigen alle;
Denn der rote Latz erhebt den gewölbeten Busen,
Schön geschnürt, und es liegt das schwarze Mieder ihr knapp an;
Sauber ist der Saum des Hemdes zur Krause gefaltet,
Und umgibt ihr das Kinn, das runde, mit reinlicher Anmut;
Frei und heiter zeigt sich des Kopfes zierliches Eirund,
Und die starken Zöpfe um silberne Nadeln gewickelt;

When the pastor had heard the praise of this girl, and her
courage,
Straightway there flowered a hope for his friend in the depth of his spirit. 120
And he was starting to ask where she might have gone at this moment
Whether she also might be on this sorrowful trek with her people.

But the druggist appeared at his side with mysterious gestures,
Plucked his clerical friend by the sleeve, and said in a whisper:
"Well, I have found her at last, from the hundreds of girls who are with her,
Just as she was described. Will you come and see for yourself? And
Take His Honor along with you; he can continue his story."
Then they turned to depart, but the magistrate could not go with them,
For at the moment his counsel was needed by some of his people.
Straightway the pastor complied with the wish of the druggist, and followed 130
Right to the hole in the fence; and the druggist cunningly pointed:
"Look at the girl who is changing the baby," he said to the pastor.
"I can easily tell it is she by the calico gown as
Well as the blue of the pillowcase brought in the bundle by Hermann.
Truly she put the gifts to good use and quickly disposed them.
These are significant tokens, and all the others are valid:
First a scarf of bright scarlet supports the curve of her bosom,
Beautifully laced and tied; and her bodice of black fits her snugly;
Neatly the hem of her blouse has been folded into a ruffle,
Framing the round of her chin with delightful precision and contrast; 140
Freely her motions display that her head is a delicate oval;
And her abundance of tresses are wound around hairpins of silver.

Sitzt sie gleich, so sehen wir doch die treffliche Größe,
Und den blauen Rock, der, vielgefaltet, vom Busen
Reichlich herunterwallt zum wohlgebildeten Knöchel.
Ohne Zweifel sie ist's. Drum kommet, damit wir
vernehmen,
Ob sie gut und tugendhaft sei, ein häusliches Mädchen.

Da versetzte der Pfarrer, mit Blicken die Sitzende prüfend:
Daß sie den Jüngling entzückt, fürwahr, es ist mir kein
Wunder;
Denn sie hält vor dem Blick des erfahrenen Mannes die
Probe.
Glücklich, wem doch Mutter Natur die rechte Gestalt gab!
Denn sie empfiehlet ihn stets, und nirgends ist er ein
Fremdling.
Jeder nahet sich gern, und jeder möchte verweilen,
Wenn die Gefälligkeit nur sich zu der Gestalt noch gesellet.
Ich versichr' euch, es ist dem Jüngling ein Mädchen gefunden,
Das ihm die künftigen Tage des Lebens herrlich erheitert,
Treu mit weiblicher Kraft durch alle Zeiten ihm beisteht.
So ein vollkommener Körper gewiß verwahrt auch die Seele
Rein, und die rüstige Jugend verspricht ein glückliches Alter.

Und es sagte darauf der Apotheker bedenklich:
Trüget doch öfter der Schein! Ich mag dem Äußern nicht
trauen;
Denn ich habe das Sprichwort so oft erprobet gefunden:
Eh du den Scheffel Salz mit dem neuen Bekannten verzehret,
Darfst du nicht leichtlich ihm trauen; dich macht die Zeit
nur gewisser,
Wie du es habest mit ihm, und wie die Freundschaft
bestehe.
Lasset uns also zuerst bei guten Leuten uns umtun,
Denen das Mädchen bekannt ist, und die uns von ihr nun
erzählen.

Even though she is sitting, we see how tall is her stature,
Also her skirt of blue, with its pleats that drop down from the bodice,
Gracefully folded and swirling right down to her beautiful ankles.
Without a doubt it is she. And so let us try to discover
If she be virtuous, good, and also a home-loving maiden."

Then the clergyman answered, while watching the girl as she sat there:
"That she enchanted the boy, to be sure, is no wonder or worry,
For in the eyes of a man of experience she is a beauty. 150
Happy the one to whom Nature has given a proper endowment,
For this will always commend him and make him generally welcome.
All are eager to meet him, and abide in his genial presence,
If to his beauty of form there be joined an agreeable spirit.
Yes, I assure you, our friend has discovered a wonderful girl for
All the rest of his life, who will cheer him and comfort him greatly,
Faithfully helping, with womanly strength, in times good and evil.
Surely a body so perfect must be a temple of goodness,
And such vigor in youth gives promise of age spent in gladness."

Then the druggist responded to this, and voiced his objection: 160
"Yes, but appearances fool us! And I am unwilling to trust them.
For I have often discovered the truth of this sensible proverb:
'Till you consume a bushel of salt with a recent acquaintance
You cannot easily trust him; for time alone makes you certain
Just how you stand with each other and whether your friendship is lasting.'
Let us, accordingly, seek for some people at first who can tell us,
Since they have known her from childhood, something about this young damsel."

Auch ich lobe die Vorsicht, versetzte der Geistliche folgend;
Frein wir doch nicht für uns! Für andere frein ist bedenklich.
Und sie gingen darauf dem wackern Richter entgegen,
Der in seinen Geschäften die Straße wieder heraufkam.
Und zu ihm sprach sogleich der kluge Pfarrer mit Vorsicht:
Sagt! wir haben ein Mädchen gesehn, das im Garten zunächst hier
Unter dem Apfelbaum sitzt, und Kindern Kleider verfertigt
Aus getragnem Kattun, der ihr vermutlich geschenkt ward.
Uns gefiel die Gestalt; sie scheint der Wackeren eine.
Saget uns, was ihr wißt; wir fragen aus löblicher Absicht.

Als in den Garten zu blicken der Richter sogleich nun herzutrat,
Sagt' er: Diese kennet ihr schon; denn wenn ich erzählte
Von der herrlichen Tat, die jene Jungfrau verrichtet,
Als sie das Schwert ergriff und sich und die Ihren beschützte—
Diese war's! Ihr seht es ihr an, sie ist rüstig geboren,
Aber so gut wie stark; denn ihren alten Verwandten
Pflegte sie bis zum Tode, da ihn der Jammer dahinriß
Über des Städtchens Not und seiner Besitzung Gefahren.
Auch, mit stillem Gemüt, hat sie die Schmerzen ertragen
Über des Bräutigams Tod, der, ein edler Jüngling, im ersten
Feuer des hohen Gedankens nach edler Freiheit zu streben,
Selbst hinging nach Paris und bald den schrecklichen Tod fand;
Denn wie zu Hause, so dort, bestritt er Willkür und Ränke.
Also sagte der Richter. Die beiden schieden und dankten,
Und der Geistliche zog ein Goldstück (das Silber des Beutels
War vor einigen Stunden von ihm schon milde verspendet,
Als er die Flüchtlinge sah in traurigen Haufen vorbeiziehn).
Und er reicht' es dem Schulzen und sagte: Teilet den Pfennig
Unter die Dürftigen aus, und Gott vermehre die Gabe!

"I am likewise in favor of prudence," responded the pastor;
"We are not suitors ourselves, and wooing for others is risky."
So then they walked toward the excellent judge, who was coming that moment, 170
Busy about his affairs, up the street once again; and the pastor
Spoke to him quietly, forming his phrases with caution and wisdom:
"Tell me, please, of the girl whom we saw just now in the garden,
Sitting there under the appletree, busy with clothing the children,
Out of cotton or calico, which I suppose has been given;
She has a noble appearance, and seems to be one of the finest:
Tell us, please, all that you know; we ask it with honest intention."

After the judge had come closer in order to look in the garden,
Straightway he said: "Why, you are acquainted with this girl already!"
For, in the story I told you of courage displayed by a maiden, 180
Who took hold of a sword and saved her people from danger,
She was the girl! You see, she was born to have vigor and courage.
But she's as good as she's strong; for did she not care for her aged
Relative, up to the time of his death, which was caused by his sorrow
Over the woe of the city, and fear for his precious possessions?
Also, with calm resignation, she bore inexpressible anguish
When her betrothed died in Paris. He was a noble young man, who,
Burning with zeal, had gone there to struggle for liberty's cause, and
Soon was brought to a terrible death; as he had done at home, he
Fought with all that was in him against intrigue and betrayal." 190
Thus spoke the judge, and the two men thanked him profusely and left him;
First though the clergyman quietly took from his pocket a goldpiece
(All of his silver was gone: he had given it all to the exiles,
When, a few hours before, he had seen their mournful procession).
This he offered the magistrate, saying: "Distribute this money
Just as is needed: may God give you more for your sorrowful people."

Doch es weigerte sich der Mann, und sagte: Wir haben
Manchen Taler gerettet und manche Kleider und Sachen,
Und ich hoffe, wir kehren zurück, noch eh es verzehrt ist.

Da versetzte der Pfarrer, und drückt' ihm das Geld
in die Hand ein:
Niemand säume zu geben in diesen Tagen, und niemand
Weigre sich anzunehmen, was ihm die Milde geboten!
Niemand weiß, wie lang er es hat, was er ruhig besitzet;
Niemand, wie lang er noch in fremden Landen umherzieht
Und des Ackers entbehrt und des Gartens, der ihn ernähret.

Ei doch! sagte darauf der Apotheker geschäftig:
Wäre mir jetzt nur Geld in der Tasche, so solltet ihr's haben,
Groß wie klein; denn viele gewiß der euren bedürfen's.
Unbeschenkt doch laß ich euch nicht, damit ihr den Willen
Sehet, woferne die Tat auch hinter dem Willen zurückbleibt.
Also sprach er, und zog den gestickten ledernen Beutel
An den Riemen hervor, worin der Toback ihm verwahrt war,
Öffnete zierlich und teilte; da fanden sich einige Pfeifen.
Klein ist die Gabe, setzt' er dazu. Da sagte der Schultheiß:
Guter Toback ist doch dem Reisenden immer willkommen.
Und es lobte darauf der Apotheker den Knaster.

Aber der Pfarrherr zog ihn hinweg, und sie schieden
vom Richter.
Eilen wir! sprach der verständige Mann; es wartet der
Jüngling
Peinlich. Er höre so schnell als möglich die fröhliche
Botschaft.

But the judge would not take it, replying: "I thank you, but
we have
Managed to save some money and clothing and other belongings.
And we hope to return before we have utterly spent it."

Then the pastor responded and forced the money upon him: 200
"None should hold back from giving these days, and no one
should either
Fail to accept for himself what a generous spirit has offered!
No one can ever be sure of how long he will hold his possessions
Or of the number of days he must wander forlorn amid strangers,
Leaving untended his fields and the garden by which he is
nourished."

"There now," the druggist remarked, with an air of busy
importance,
"Had I but money in pocket, you would be welcome to take it:
Bills or coins, I assure you, because your people are needy.
But, sir, I'll not say farewell without a token of kindness.
Though the action falls short, you can see my intention was kindly." 210
These were his words as he drew from his pocket a purse made
of leather,
Neatly embroidered, in which he had packed his favorite tobacco;
Opened and passed it around, with an air of graceful distinction.
There were some pipes in the packet. "It's not much to give
you," he added.
Then the magistrate answered: "Every traveler is pleased when
Good tobacco is offered." The druggist then praised his canaster.

But the pastor then drew him away, and they took their
departure.
"Let us make haste!" said the sensible pastor, "for Hermann
is waiting
Anxiously: we must tell him at once of the news we have
brought him."

Und sie eilten und kamen und fanden den Jüngling gelehnet
An den Wagen unter den Linden. Die Pferde zerstampften
Wild den Rasen; er hielt sie im Zaum, und stand in
Gedanken,
Blickte still vor sich hin und sah die Freunde nicht eher,
Bis sie kommend ihn riefen und fröhliche Zeichen ihm
gaben.
Schon von ferne begann der Apotheker zu sprechen;
Doch sie traten näher hinzu. Da faßte der Pfarrherr
Seine Hand, und sprach und nahm dem Gefährten das
Wort weg:
Heil dir, junger Mann! dein treues Auge, dein treues
Herz hat richtig gewählt! Glück dir und dem Weibe der
Jugend!
Deiner ist sie wert; drum komm und wende den Wagen,
Daß wir fahrend sogleich die Ecke des Dorfes erreichen,
Um sie werben und bald nach Hause führen die Gute.

Aber der Jüngling stand, und ohne Zeichen der Freude
Hört' er die Worte des Boten, die himmlisch waren und
tröstlich,
Seufzete tief und sprach: Wir kamen mit eilendem Fuhrwerk,
Und wir ziehen vielleicht beschämt und langsam nach
Hause;
Denn hier hat mich, seitdem ich warte, die Sorge befallen,
Argwohn und Zweifel und alles, was nur ein liebendes Herz
kränkt.
Glaubt ihr, wenn wir nur kommen, so werde das Mädchen
uns folgen,
Weil wir reich sind, aber sie arm und vertrieben einherzieht?
Armut selbst macht stolz, die unverdiente. Genügsam
Scheint das Mädchen und tätig; und so gehört ihr die
Welt an.

And they hurried, and came, and discovered the young man a-leaning 220
There on the carriage under the lime-trees. The horses were stamping
Restlessly on the green grass; Hermann was holding them in, but
Seemed to be lost in reflection, staring in front of him, blankly.
Nor did he notice his friends till, approaching, they called him by name and
Gestured to indicate triumph. Even afar did the druggist
Start to explain what had happened, but when they came closer the pastor
Reached for the hand of the youth and interrupted his comrade.
"Bravo for you, my young friend! Your vision is clear and your heart is
True: you have chosen most wisely! May you and the wife of your youth be
Happy and blessed, for she is worthy of you! Therefore come, and 230
Turn the horses around: let us speed to the edge of the village,
There to ask for her hand, and quickly return with the maiden."

Hermann, however, stood still, and his face grew not brighter on hearing
All that the messenger said (though his words were heavenly comfort).
Yes, he drew a deep sigh, and exclaimed: "How quickly the carriage
Brought us here, but how likely that we shall return to our home in
Shame and with slowness. For I have bethought me since I have been waiting.
Doubt and suspicion and anguish, all the ills of a loving
Heart have befallen me. Think you we have but to come and the girl will
Follow us simply because we are rich, while she is in exile? 240
Poverty makes a girl proud, if she hasn't deserved it. Contented
She seems to be, and active; and so the world is her oyster.

Glaubt ihr, es sei ein Weib von solcher Schönheit und Sitte
Aufgewachsen, um nie den guten Jüngling zu reizen?
Glaubt ihr, sie habe bis jetzt ihr Herz verschlossen der
Liebe?
Fahret nicht rasch bis hinan; wir möchten zu unsrer
Beschämung
Sachte die Pferde herum nach Hause lenken. Ich fürchte,
Irgend ein Jüngling besitzt dies Herz, und die wackere
Hand hat
Eingeschlagen und schon dem Glücklichen Treue
versprochen.
Ach! da steh ich vor ihr mit meinem Antrag beschämet.

Ihn zu trösten, öffnete drauf der Pfarrer den Mund schon;
Doch es fiel der Gefährte mit seiner gesprächigen Art ein:
Freilich! so wären wir nicht vor Zeiten verlegen gewesen,
Da ein jedes Geschäft nach seiner Weise vollbracht ward.
Hatten die Eltern die Braut für ihren Sohn sich ersehen,
Ward zuvörderst ein Freund vom Hause vertraulich
gerufen;
Diesen sandte man dann als Freiersmann zu den Eltern
Der erkorenen Braut, der dann in stattlichem Putze
Sonntags etwa nach Tische den würdigen Bürger besuchte,
Freundliche Worte mit ihm im allgemeinen zuvörderst
Wechselnd, und klug das Gespräch zu lenken und wenden
verstehend.
Endlich nach langem Umschweif ward auch der Tochter
erwähnet,
Rühmlich, und rühmlich des Manns und des Hauses, von
dem man gesandt war.
Kluge Leute merkten die Absicht; der kluge Gesandte
Merkte den Willen gar bald, und konnte sich weiter
erklären.
Lehnte den Antrag man ab, so war auch ein Korb nicht
verdrießlich.
Aber gelang es denn auch, so war der Freiersmann immer

Think you, a maiden of beauty and virtue like hers could have
come to
Womanhood, never arousing desire in the heart of a man, or
Think you, her heart till this moment is free from the passion
of love? O
Let us not speed there so rashly! We might be embarrassed and
forced to
Turn the horses around and go home, for I fear that her heart is
Given already to someone, whose hand she has loyally shaken,
Promising him her fidelity now and forever; and there I
Stand with my offer, ashamed and covered with deepest 250
confusion."

Just as the pastor was opening his mouth to comfort poor
Hermann,
Quickly the drugggist broke in, in his usual garrulous manner:
"Yes, to be sure! Long ago we would *not* have been shamed or
embarrassed,
For in the past every task was properly brought to completion.
Once the parents had chosen a bride for their son, the very
First thing they did was to summon in secret a friend of the family;
Him they would send as a gobetween then to the home of the
maiden.
He would get dressed in all of his best, and, possibly, after
Dinner on Sunday, would visit the honorable burgher and speak of
Matters in general, just in a friendly, casual manner, 260
Cleverly steering the talk in the way he wanted to steer it;
Finally, after the prelude, he came to mention the daughter,
Honoring her, and the man, and the family who sent him
to woo her.
Parents with tact would be quick to guess his intention, and
likewise
Tactfully then the envoy would sense their desire and explain his
Fullest intention in coming. But if they rejected the offer
No one was hurt or offended; but if the mission succeeded,

In dem Hause der Erste bei jedem häuslichen Feste;
Denn es erinnerte sich durch's ganze Leben das Ehpaar,
Daß die geschickte Hand den ersten Knoten geschlungen.
Jetzt ist aber das alles, mit andern guten Gebräuchen,
Aus der Mode gekommen, und jeder freit für sich selber.
Nehme denn jeglicher auch den Korb mit eigenen Händen,
Der ihm etwa beschert ist, und stehe beschämt vor dem Mädchen!

Sei es, wie ihm auch sei! versetzte der Jüngling, der kaum auf
Alle die Worte gehört, und schon sich im stillen entschlossen:
Selber geh ich und will mein Schicksal selber erfahren
Aus dem Munde des Mädchens, zu dem ich das größte Vertrauen
Hege, das irgend ein Mensch nur je zu dem Weibe gehegt hat.
Was sie sagt, das ist gut, es ist vernünftig, das weiß ich.
Soll ich sie auch zum letztenmal sehn, so will ich noch einmal
Diesem offenen Blick des schwarzen Auges begegnen;
Drück ich sie nie an das Herz, so will ich die Brust und die Schultern
Einmal noch sehn, die mein Arm so sehr zu umschließen begehret;
Will den Mund noch sehen, von dem ein Kuß und das Ja mich
Glücklich macht auf ewig, das Nein mich auf ewig zerstöret.
Aber laßt mich allein! Ihr sollt nicht warten. Begebet
Euch zu Vater und Mutter zurück, damit sie erfahren,
Daß sich der Sohn nicht geirrt, und daß es wert ist das Mädchen.
Und so laßt mich allein! Den Fußweg über den Hügel
An dem Birnbaum hin, und unsern Weinberg hinunter,
Geh ich näher nach Hause zurück. O, daß ich die Traute
Freudig und schnell heimführte! Vielleicht auch schleich ich alleine
Jene Pfade nach Haus, und betrete froh sie nicht wieder.

Honor was paid to the envoy at every feast of the family,
For through all of their lives the couple would gladly remember
How the skill of his hand had tied the knot of their marriage. 270
This, however, with other fine customs, is now really out of
Fashion, and each one arranges his marriage just as he likes it.
So then, let everyone take his refusal into his own hands,
If a refusal is given, and face the girl in confusion."

"That may very well be!" responded the youth, who had listened
Only with half of his mind, and had secretly made a decision.
"I am going myself, and I myself will receive from
Her lips my fate. For, I assure you, I trust her far more than
Ever a man has trusted a woman. Whatever she says will
Surely be reasonable, surely be good—I am certain as *can* be. 280
If it be fated for me to see her no more I must see her
This once, face the ingenuous glance of her beautiful eyes; and
If I may never embrace her, I simply must see once again her
Shoulders and breast, which I long to enfold in my arms; once again I
Must see the lips whose assent and whose kiss would delight me forever,
As indeed a refusal, a No, would forever destroy me.
Now you must leave me alone. Do not wait, but quickly return to
Father and mother, waiting at home, that they may be sure that
Hermann, their son, has committed no error in choosing this woman.
Now please leave me alone, and I will return by the footpath 290
Over the hill past the peartree and down through the vineyard. For thus I
Shorten the way and arrive as quickly as you do. And would that
She, my belovèd, came with me, joyful and swift, but
Soon must walk there alone on the path, in sorrow forever."

Also sprach er und gab dem geistlichen Herrn die Zügel,
Der verständig sie faßte, die schäumenden Rosse
beherrschend,
Schnell den Wagen bestieg und den Sitz des Führers besetzte.

Aber du zaudertest noch, vorsichtiger Nachbar,
und sagtest:
Gerne vertrau ich, mein Freund, euch Seel und Geist und
Gemüt an;
Aber Leib und Gebein ist nicht zum besten verwahret,
Wenn die geistliche Hand der weltlichen Zügel sich anmaßt.
Doch du lächeltest drauf, verständiger Pfarrer, und sagtest:
Sitzet nur ein, und getrost vertraut mir den Leib, wie die
Seele;
Denn geschickt ist die Hand schon lange, den Zügel zu
führen,
Und das Auge geübt, die künstlichste Wendung zu treffen.
Denn wir waren in Straßburg gewohnt den Wagen zu lenken,
Als ich den jungen Baron dahin begleitete; täglich
Rollte der Wagen, geleitet von mir, das hallende Tor durch,
Staubige Wege hinaus, bis fern zu den Auen und Linden,
Mitten durch Scharen des Volks, das mit Spazieren den
Tag lebt.

Halb getröstet bestieg darauf der Nachbar den Wagen,
Saß wie einer, der sich zum weislichen Sprunge bereitet;
Und die Hengste rannten nach Hause, begierig des Stalles.
Aber die Wolke des Staubs quoll unter den mächtigen Hufen.
Lange noch stand der Jüngling, und sah den Staub sich
erheben,
Sah den Staub sich zerstreun; so stand er ohne Gedanken.

Thus spoke the youth and transferred the reins to the hands of the pastor,
Who with finesse took them up, controlling the spirited horses.
Quickly he mounted the carriage, and sat in the seat of the coachman.

But, O most cautious of neighbors, you paused for a moment, and said then:
"Gladly, my friend, I entrust to your care my soul and my spirit,
But our lives and our bodies do not find the surest protection 300
When a clergyman's hands are controlling secular horses!"
But you smiled at him then, intelligent pastor, and answered:
"Just take your seat, for your body with me is as safe as your soul is.
For I have long been accustomed to driving a carriage; my hand and
Eye are practised and trained in the finest nuances of driving.
For we accustomed ourselves in Straßburg to driving a carriage;
When I was there as the baron's companion and mentor, why, daily
Through the echoing gateway the carriage I drove came a-rolling
Onto the highway and over the dusty lanes, to the distant
Meadows and trees, through the crowds who were spending the day in the country." 310

Comforted only by half, the neighbor mounted the carriage,
Sitting like one who is ready to jump if caution requires it.
Swiftly the stallions sped toward the city, seeking their stable.
And from the beat of their hooves a dust cloud arose on the roadway.
Hermann stood there a long time and watched the dust in its rising,
Watched, as it settled again; he stood there, but thought was not in him.

VII

ERATO

Dorothea

Wie der wandernde Mann, der vor dem Sinken der Sonne
Sie noch einmal ins Auge, die schnellverschwindende, faßte,
Dann im dunkeln Gebüsch, dann vor der düsteren Felswand
Schweben siehet ihr Bild; wohin er die Blicke nur wendet,
Eilet es vor und glänzt und schwankt in herrlichen Farben:
So bewegte vor Hermann die liebliche Bildung des Mädchens
Sanft sich vorbei, und schien dem Pfad ins Getreide zu folgen.
Aber er fuhr aus dem staunenden Traum auf, wendete langsam
Nach dem Dorfe sich zu, und staunte wieder; denn wieder
Kam ihm die hohe Gestalt des herrlichen Mädchens entgegen.
Fest betrachtet er sie; es war kein Scheinbild, sie war es
Selber. Den größeren Krug und einen kleinern am Henkel
Tragend in jeglicher Hand: so schritt sie geschäftig zum Brunnen.
Und er ging ihr freudig entgegen. Es gab ihm ihr Anblick
Mut und Kraft; er sprach zu seiner Verwunderten also:
Find ich dich, wackeres Mädchen, so bald aufs neue beschäftigt,
Hülfreich andern zu sein und gern zu erquicken die Menschen?
Sag, warum kommst du allein zum Quell, der doch so entfernt liegt,
Da sich andere doch mit dem Wasser des Dorfes begnügen?
Freilich ist dies von besonderer Kraft und lieblich zu kosten.
Jener Kranken bringst du es wohl, die du treulich gerettet?

VII

ERATO

Dorothea

Just as a wanderer watches the sun in its westerly sinking,
Sees it rapidly vanishing, looks once more at its splendor,
Then on the darkening shrubs and the face of the cliff high
above him,
Watches its image suspended; it constantly hurries before him,
Gleaming and flick'ring in colors magnificent, ever receding;
Thus before Hermann the image and form of the girl was
receding,
Seeming to move gently past him and taking the path to the
wheatfield.
But from his dream he awakened, and started to turn toward the
village,
When he was struck with amazement; for there approached him
the stately
Form of the beautiful girl. He looked at her steadily; this was 10
Not an illusion at all; it was Dorothea in person,
Carrying jugs, a large one and small one, each by the handle,
One in each hand; and thus she stepped briskly up to the water.
And he approached her with rapture; the sight of her gave him
new courage,
And his purpose was strengthened. He said, as she stood there
astonished:
"So, here I find you once more, devoted to serving your people,
Bringing them cooling refreshment and cheerfully helping
the needy.
Tell me: why do you come here alone to a spring so far distant,
When the others are willing to drink from the springs in the village?
(Though this water is good to the taste and especially healthful.) 20
You are bringing it now to the invalid whom you once rescued?"

Freundlich begrüßte sogleich das gute Mädchen den Jüngling,
Sprach: So ist schon hier der Weg mir zum Brunnen belohnet,
Da ich finde den Guten, der uns so vieles gereicht hat;
Denn der Anblick des Gebers ist, wie die Gaben, erfreulich.
Kommt und sehet doch selber, wer eure Milde genossen,
Und empfanget den ruhigen Dank von allen Erquickten.
Daß ihr aber sogleich vernehmet, warum ich gekommen,
Hier zu schöpfen, wo rein und unablässig der Quell fließt,
Sag ich euch dies: es haben die unvorsichtigen Menschen
Alles Wasser getrübt im Dorfe, mit Pferden und Ochsen
Gleich durchwatend den Quell, der Wasser bringt den Bewohnern.
Und so haben sie auch mit Waschen und Reinigen alle
Tröge des Dorfes beschmutzt und alle Brunnen besudelt;
Denn ein jeglicher denkt nur, sich selbst und das nächste Bedürfnis
Schnell zu befriedgen und rasch, und nicht des Folgenden denkt er.

Also sprach sie und war die breiten Stufen hinunter
Mit dem Begleiter gelangt; und auf das Mäuerchen setzten
Beide sich nieder des Quells. Sie beugte sich über, zu schöpfen;
Und er faßte den anderen Krug, und beugte sich über.
Und sie sahen gespiegelt ihr Bild in der Bläue des Himmels
Schwanken, und nickten sich zu, und grüßten sich freundlich im Spiegel.
Laß mich trinken, sagte darauf der heitere Jüngling;
Und sie reicht' ihm den Krug. Dann ruhten sie beide, vertraulich
Auf die Gefäße gelehnt; sie aber sagte zum Freunde:
Sage, wie find ich dich hier? und ohne Wagen und Pferde

Pleasantly then the good maiden saluted Hermann, with
promptness,
Saying: "My walk to the spring is even at this point rewarded,
Since I encounter the man whose kindness has helped us so greatly.
Seeing the giver is even more welcome than seeing his gifts, so
Come then, and see for yourself the people your goodness has
aided;
Come and receive hearty thanks for all that delightful
refreshment.
But I will tell you at once exactly why I have come here,
Here to the spring to draw water, where it flows swiftly and purely.
There in the village the crowd, with incredible negligence, rudely 30
Sullied the water, permitting their horses and oxen to wade
through
Even the spring which provides the village with water. And also
Every trough in the village is fouled with washing and bathing,
And every fountain is dirtied. For each intends only to fill his
Own immediate need as fast as he's able, and never
Thinks of the others, or what may be needed by those who
will follow."

Thus having spoken she came with her escort down the broad
staircase.
Both of them seated themselves on the little wall by the spring. And
She bent over the surface, intending to draw out some water,
He, taking hold of the larger receptacle, bent over also. 40
There in the blue of the sky they beheld their images mirrored,
Rocking, and in the mirror, they nodded and smiled at each other.
"Give me a drink!" said Hermann cheerfully then to the maiden,
And she passed him the pitcher. They rested then, leaning
in comfort
Each on his pitcher. The maiden addressed him in friendliest
manner:
"Tell me, why are you here? And where are your horses and
carriage?

Ferne vom Ort, wo ich erst dich gesehn? wie bist du gekommen?

Denkend schaute Hermann zur Erde; dann hob er die Blicke
Ruhig gegen sie auf, und sah ihr freundlich ins Auge,
Fühlte sich still und getrost. Jedoch ihr von Liebe zu sprechen,
Wär ihm unmöglich gewesen; ihr Auge blickte nicht Liebe,
Aber hellen Verstand, und gebot verständig zu reden.
Und er faßte sich schnell, und sagte traulich zum Mädchen:
Laß mich reden, mein Kind, und deine Fragen erwidern.
Deinetwegen kam ich hierher! was soll ich's verbergen?
Denn ich lebe beglückt mit beiden liebenden Eltern,
Denen ich treulich das Haus und die Güter helfe verwalten,
Als der einzige Sohn, und unsre Geschäfte sind vielfach.
Alle Felder besorg ich: der Vater waltet im Hause
Fleißig; die tätige Mutter belebt im Ganzen die Wirtschaft.
Aber du hast gewiß auch erfahren, wie sehr das Gesinde
Bald durch Leichtsinn und bald durch Untreu plaget die Hausfrau,
Immer sie nötigt zu wechseln und Fehler um Fehler zu tauschen.
Lange wünschte die Mutter daher sich ein Mädchen im Hause,
Das mit der Hand nicht allein, das auch mit dem Herzen ihr hülfe,
An der Tochter Statt, der leider frühe verlornen.
Nun, als ich heut am Wagen dich sah, in froher Gewandtheit,
Sah die Stärke des Arms und die volle Gesundheit der Glieder,
Als ich die Worte vernahm, die verständigen, war ich betroffen,
Und ich eilte nach Hause, den Eltern und Freunden die Fremde
Rühmend nach ihrem Verdienst. Nun komm ich dir aber zu sagen,

How, so far from the place where I saw you at first, did you get here?"

Thoughtfully Hermann gazed at the ground, then lifted his eyes and
Looked in her face, quite calmly, and showing his tender affection,
Feeling peaceful and cheerful. Yet he was not at all able 50
Now to mention his love, for her manner betokened not love, but
Keenest intelligence. Reasonable discourse was clearly in order.
So he controlled himself quickly and cordially spoke to the maiden.
"Let me answer, my child, and explain my reason for coming.
You are the reason I came! For why should I try to conceal it?
For I live with affectionate parents, and live with them gladly,
Faithfully helping them manage the inn and all our possessions;
I am their only son, and our business is varied and taxing.
My work is care of the land, while my father's concern is the household
Constantly; mother enlivens and manages everything wisely. 60
But you have certainly heard of annoyance suffered by housewives,
Which results from the foolish or faithless behavior of servants,
Causing them ever to switch, thus exchanging error for error.
That is the reason my mother has wanted a girl in the household
Who would help her not only with hands but also with heart, in
Place of the daughter who died long ago, to her infinite sorrow.
Well, when I saw you today from the carriage, so skillful and cheerful,
Saw the strength of your arm, and the marvelous health of your body,
When I heard your intelligent speech, I was pleased beyond measure,
And I hurried back home to my friends and my parents to tell them 70
All about your excellent merits, and now I have come to

Was sie wünschen, wie ich.—Verzeih mir die stotternde
Rede.

Scheuet euch nicht, so sagte sie drauf, das Weitre zu
sprechen;
Ihr beleidigt mich nicht, ich hab es dankbar empfunden.
Sagt es nur grad heraus; mich kann das Wort nicht
erschrecken:
Dingen möchtet ihr mich als Magd für Vater und Mutter,
Zu versehen das Haus, das wohlerhalten euch dasteht;
Und ihr glaubet an mir ein tüchtiges Mädchen zu finden,
Zu der Arbeit geschickt und nicht von rohem Gemüte.
Euer Antrag war kurz; so soll die Antwort auch kurz sein.
Ja, ich gehe mit euch, und folge dem Rufe des Schicksals.
Meine Pflicht ist erfüllt, ich habe die Wöchnerin wieder
Zu den Ihren gebracht, sie freuen sich alle der Rettung;
Schon sind die meisten beisammen, die übrigen werden sich
finden.
Alle denken gewiß, in kurzen Tagen zur Heimat
Wiederzukehren; so pflegt sich stets der Vertriebne zu
schmeicheln;
Aber ich täusche mich nicht mit leichter Hoffnung in diesen
Traurigen Tagen, die uns noch traurige Tage versprechen:
Denn gelöst sind die Bande der Welt; wer knüpfet sie
wieder
Als allein nur die Not, die höchste, die uns bevorsteht!
Kann ich im Hause des würdigen Manns mich, dienend,
ernähren
Unter den Augen der trefflichen Frau, so tu ich es gerne;
Denn ein wanderndes Mädchen ist immer von schwankendem
Rufe.
Ja, ich gehe mit euch, sobald ich die Krüge den Freunden
Wiedergebracht und noch mir den Segen der Guten
erbeten.
Kommt! Ihr müsset sie sehen, und mich von ihnen
empfangen.

Tell you their wishes and mine. Pray excuse my awkward
expression!"

"Be not embarrassed," she answered, "continue to speak of
your offer.
Nothing you say can offend me. Your offer is gracious and welcome.
Tell me your meaning straight out, for I am not frightened to
hear it:
You would like to engage me to serve as maid for your parents
And to care for the house and keep it in best of condition.
You have discovered in me a competent, trustworthy servant,
Skilled in her work and friendly, and blessed with a good
disposition.
Short and concise was your offer, and my reply will be like it: 80
Yes, I will go with you now; I shall follow where destiny calls me.
Here my duty is done; the new mother is back with her people.
All are pleased with their rescue and most of them now are
together.
Soon the others will join them. Everyone thinks it is sure that
They will return to their homes before many days have elapsed, but
This is the way in which exiles are used to deceive themselves
often.
But in these sorrowful days I am not deceived by a hope so
Specious, since I am certain that more of such days will ensue, for
All the bonds of the world are unloosened, and who will
retie them?
Only necessity dire, such as that we are facing. If *I* can 90
Serve in the house of a praiseworthy man and earn my support by
Helping his excellent wife, I will do it with thanks and with
gladness,
For an itinerant girl has always a poor reputation.
Yes, I will go with you now, and as soon as these pitchers of water
Can be brought to my people, I'll ask them to give me their blessing.
Come, you must pay your respects, and ask their permission
to take me."

Fröhlich hörte der Jüngling des willigen Mädchens Entschließung,
Zweifelnd, ob er ihr nun die Wahrheit sollte gestehen.
Aber es schien ihm das beste zu sein, in dem Wahn sie zu lassen,
In sein Haus sie zu führen, zu werben um Liebe nur dort erst.
Ach! und den goldenen Ring erblickt' er am Finger des Mädchens;
Und so ließ er sie sprechen, und horchte fleißig den Worten.

Laßt uns, fuhr sie nun fort, zurücke kehren! Die Mädchen
Werden immer getadelt, die lange beim Brunnen verweilen;
Und doch ist es am rinnenden Quell so lieblich zu schwätzen.
Also standen sie auf und schauten beide noch einmal
In den Brunnen zurück, und süßes Verlangen ergriff sie.

Schweigend nahm sie darauf die beiden Krüge beim Henkel,
Stieg die Stufen hinan, und Hermann folgte der Lieben.
Einen Krug verlangt' er von ihr, die Bürde zu teilen.
Laßt ihn, sprach sie; es trägt sich besser die gleichere Last so.
Und der Herr, der künftig befiehlt, er soll mir nicht dienen.
Seht mich so ernst nicht an, als wäre mein Schicksal bedenklich!
Dienen lerne bei Zeiten das Weib nach ihrer Bestimmung;
Denn durch Dienen allein gelangt sie endlich zum Herrschen,
Zu der verdienten Gewalt, die doch ihr im Hause gehöret.
Dienet die Schwester dem Bruder doch früh, sie dienet den Eltern,
Und ihr Leben ist immer ein ewiges Gehen und Kommen,
Oder ein Heben und Tragen, Bereiten und Schaffen für andre.
Wohl ihr, wenn sie daran sich gewöhnt, daß kein Weg ihr zu sauer

Hermann joyfully heard Dorothea's willing acceptance,
Wondering whether the moment had come to tell her the truth, but
Still it seemed to him wisest to leave her in her delusion,
And to take her straight home, and only to sue for her love then. 100
And, alas, he beheld on her finger the circlet of gold, and
So he allowed her to talk, and listened with closest attention.

"Let us," continued the maiden, "return to my people! The girls who
Stay at the fountain too long are always deserving of censure;
Yet it is sweet to sit here and talk by the murmuring fountain."
So they stood up and both looked again at the sparkling reflection
There in the well, and were seized by a secret and passionate yearning.

Then, without saying a word, she took hold of the jugs by the handles;
Quickly she went up the stairs, and then Hermann followed his darling.
Then he besought Dorothea that he might carry a pitcher. 110
"No," she replied, "they are easy to carry if they are balanced.
And the master, who soon will give orders, must *not* help his servant.
Do not regard me so gravely, as if my fate were unpleasant!
Women should learn in their youth that fate has designed them for service.
For through service alone can a woman attain to dominion,
To the merited power which should be hers in the household.
Does not a sister perform her due service for brother and parents?
All of her life she is busily, constantly coming and going,
Carrying, lifting, preparing, and generally doing for others.
Happy is she if she learns that no errand is ever too bitter, 120

Wird, und die Stunden der Nacht ihr sind wie die Stunden des Tages,
Daß ihr niemals die Arbeit zu klein und die Nadel zu fein dünkt,
Daß sie sich ganz vergißt und leben mag nur in andern!
Denn als Mutter, fürwahr, bedarf sie der Tugenden alle,
Wenn der Säugling die Krankende weckt und Nahrung begehret
Von der Schwachen, und so zu Schmerzen Sorgen sich häufen.
Zwanzig Männer verbunden ertrügen nicht diese Beschwerde,
Und sie sollen es nicht; doch sollen sie dankbar es einsehn.

Also sprach sie, und war, mit ihrem stillen Begleiter,
Durch den Garten gekommen, bis an die Tenne der Scheune,
Wo die Wöchnerin lag, die sie froh mit den Töchtern verlassen,
Jenen geretteten Mädchen, den schönen Bildern der Unschuld.
Beide traten hinein; und von der anderen Seite
Trat, ein Kind an jeglicher Hand, der Richter zugleich ein.
Diese waren bisher der jammernden Mutter verloren;
Aber gefunden hatte sie nun im Gewimmel der Alte.
Und sie sprangen mit Lust, die liebe Mutter zu grüßen,
Sich des Bruders zu freun, des unbekannten Gespielen!
Auf Dorotheen sprangen sie dann und grüßten sie freundlich,
Brot verlangend und Obst, vor allem aber zu trinken.
Und sie reichte das Wasser herum. Da tranken die Kinder,
Und die Wöchnerin trank, mit den Töchtern, so trank auch der Richter.
Alle waren geletzt, und lobten das herrliche Wasser;
Säuerlich war's und erquicklich, gesund zu trinken den Menschen.

Da versetzte das Mädchen mit ernsten Blicken und sagte:

And that the hours of darkness should be like the hours
of daylight;
Never is housework too petty or needles too fine for her liking.
She must simply forget her own self and live but for others!
For, as a mother, in truth, she must have ev'ry one of these
virtues.
When she is sick and her baby awakes she must suckle him, even
Though she be weak; thus to pain is added anxiety often.
Twenty men put together could not endure such harassment.
Nor indeed should they; yet they *should* understand and be
grateful."

Thus she spoke, and had come by now with her silent
companion
Through the garden and up to the threshing floor of the barn, for 130
There the happy new mother was lying, surrounded by daughters.
These were the girls she had rescued, the very models of virtue.
Both of them entered the room, and from the opposite side came,
Leading a child by each hand, the magistrate, at the same moment.
These were the children the agonized mother had lost, whom the
judge had
Now discovered astray in the turbulent crowd of the exiles.
Joyful, they sprang to the side of their idolized mother, to
greet her,
Pleased by the thought of a brother, a playmate as yet unfamiliar.
Then they fondly embraced Dorothea and greeted her warmly,
Asking for bread and for fruit, but most especially for water. 140
And she gave them the water. The children drank, and the mother,
Also the daughters, and even the magistrate drank it, and all were
Cooled by the wonderful water, and praised its freshness and
savor.
Slightly acid it was, but refreshing and healthful for humans.

Then the maiden spoke up with serious mien, and addressed
them:

Freunde, dieses ist wohl das letztemal, daß ich den Krug euch
Führe zum Munde, daß ich die Lippen mit Wasser euch netze:
Aber wenn euch fortan am heißen Tage der Trunk labt,
Wenn ihr im Schatten der Ruh und der reinen Quellen genießet,
Dann gedenket auch mein und meines freundlichen Dienstes,
Den ich aus Liebe mehr als aus Verwandtschaft geleistet.
Was ihr mir Gutes erzeigt', erkenn ich durch's künftige Leben.
Ungern laß ich euch zwar; doch jeder ist diesmal dem andern
Mehr zur Last als zum Trost, und alle müssen wir endlich
Uns im fremden Lande zerstreun, wenn die Rückkehr versagt ist.
Seht, hier steht der Jüngling, dem wir die Gaben verdanken,
Diese Hülle des Kinds und jene willkommene Speise.
Dieser kommt und wirbt, in seinem Haus mich zu sehen,
Daß ich diene daselbst den reichen trefflichen Eltern;
Und ich schlag es nicht ab; denn überall dienet das Mädchen,
Und ihr wäre zur Last, bedient im Hause zu ruhen.
Also folg ich ihm gern; er scheint ein verständiger Jüngling,
Und so werden die Eltern es sein, wie Reichen geziemet.
Darum lebet nun wohl, geliebte Freundin, und freuet
Euch des lebendigen Säuglings, der schon so gesund euch anblickt.
Drücket ihr ihn an die Brust in diesen farbigen Wickeln,
O, so gedenket des Jünglings, des guten, der sie uns reichte,
Und der künftig auch mich, die Eure, nähret und kleidet.
Und ihr, trefflicher Mann, so sprach sie gewendet zum Richter,
Habet Dank, daß ihr Vater mir wart in mancherlei Fällen.

Und sie kniete darauf zur guten Wöchnerin nieder,

"Friends, this is doubtless the last opportunity ever for me to
Bring you the jug from the well, or to moisten your lips with this water.
But, when the weather is warm, and water refreshes you henceforth,
When in the shade you are resting and taking a drink from the fountain,
Think then, I beg you, of me, and the friendly service I did you, 150
Which I performed from motives of tenderness rather than kinship.
I shall remember in future forever the good you have done me.
I am reluctant to leave you, but each of us seems to the other
More of a weight than a comfort; and we all must eventually scatter,
If a return to our homeland is finally and firmly denied us.
See, here stands the youth who recently gave of his bounty
Much needed clothes for the children, and food we have gratefully eaten.
He has come and besought me to live in his home, so that I may
Serve his prosperous, excellent parents, and help them with housework.
I shall accept his proposal; for everywhere maidens must serve, and 160
They would be very unhappy if they were served and not serving.
So I shall follow him gladly. He seems like a sensible fellow.
And his parents are probably sensible also, befitting their riches.
Therefore farewell, my dear friend, and rejoice in your wonderful baby,
Who is already directing a healthy look toward his mother.
When you embrace him in future, dressed in these colorful diapers,
O, just think of the kind young man who bestowed them upon us,
Who from this moment will furnish me also with food and with clothing."
Then, as she turned, and she said to the judge, "O excellent man, I
Thank you for being a father to me in all sorts of troubles." 170

Then Dorothea knelt down and embraced the weeping new mother,

Küßte die weinende Frau, und vernahm des Segens Gelispel.
Aber du sagtest indes, ehrwürdiger Richter, zu Hermann:
Billig seid ihr, o Freund, zu den guten Wirten zu zählen,
Die mit tüchtigen Menschen den Haushalt zu führen
bedacht sind.
Denn ich habe wohl oft gesehn, daß man Rinder und Pferde,
So wie Schafe, genau bei Tausch und Handel betrachtet;
Aber den Menschen, der alles erhält, wenn er tüchtig
und gut ist,
Und der alles zerstreut und zerstört durch falsches Beginnen,
Diesen nimmt man nur so auf Glück und Zufall ins Haus ein,
Und bereuet zu spät ein übereiltes Entschließen.
Aber es scheint, ihr versteht's; denn ihr habt ein Mädchen
erwählet,
Euch zu dienen im Haus und euren Eltern, das brav ist.
Haltet sie wohl! Ihr werdet, so lang sie der Wirtschaft
sich annimmt,
Nicht die Schwester vermissen, noch eure Eltern die Tochter.

Viele kamen indes, der Wöchnerin nahe Verwandte,
Manches bringend und ihr die bessere Wohnung verkündend.
Alle vernahmen des Mädchens Entschluß, und segneten
Hermann
Mit bedeutenden Blicken und mit besondern Gedanken.
Denn so sagte wohl eine zur andern flüchtig ans Ohr hin:
Wenn aus dem Herrn ein Bräutigam wird, so ist sie geborgen.
Hermann faßte darauf sie bei der Hand an und sagte:
Laß uns gehen; es neigt sich der Tag und fern ist das
Städtchen.
Lebhaft gesprächig umarmten darauf Dorotheen die Weiber.
Hermann zog sie hinweg; noch viele Grüße befahl sie.
Aber da fielen die Kinder, mit Schrein und entsetzlichem
Weinen,
Ihr in die Kleider, und wollten die zweite Mutter
nicht lassen.

Kissed her and heard how she faintly and fervently whispered
a blessing.
But in the meantime, honorable magistrate, you addressed Hermann:
"You, my young friend, can surely be counted among the
best landlords,
Who are anxious to manage their households with competent
helpers.
For I have often observed that cattle and horses are tested
Closely, as also are sheep, before they are purchased or traded.
But a person who keeps things in shape if he is efficient,
And if he starts things the wrong way produces waste and
destruction,
Is selected at random, and given a place in the household; 180
When it is too late to mend, they will rue the hasty decision.
But, it seems, *you* are able to judge, for I see you have chosen
One to serve in your household who will be good for your parents.
Cherish her fondly! As long as *she* is in charge of the
household
You will not lack a sister, and your parents will have a
fine daughter."

Meanwhile many were coming with presents, the new mother's
kinfolk,
Bringing the news of a better abode for herself and her baby.
Everyone heard of the girl's resolution, and kept blessing Hermann,
Giving him meaningful looks and drawing important conclusions.
One girl furtively whispered these words in the ear of another: 190
"If he should change from employer to bridegroom her
fortune is certain."
Hermann then took hold of her hand and said to her softly:
"Let us depart, for our city is distant, and evening is coming."
Then the women embraced Dorothea with noisy affection.
Hermann drew her away, as she said her farewells to the others.
But then the children took hold of her clothing with terrible weeping,
Hating to let her depart, for she had been like a mother.

Aber ein und die andre der Weiber sagte gebietend:
Stille, Kinder! sie geht in die Stadt, und bringt euch
des guten
Zuckerbrotes genug, das euch der Bruder bestellte,
Als der Storch ihn jüngst beim Zuckerbäcker vorbeitrug,
Und ihr sehet sie bald mit den schön vergoldeten Deuten.
Und so ließen die Kinder sie los, und Hermann entriß sie
Noch den Umarmungen kaum und den fernewinkenden
Tüchern.

VIII

MELPOMENE

Hermann und Dorothea

Also gingen die zwei entgegen der sinkenden Sonne,
Die in Wolken sich tief, gewitterdrohend, verhüllte,
Aus dem Schleier, bald hier bald dort, mit glühenden
Blicken
Strahlend über das Feld die ahnungsvolle Beleuchtung.
Möge das drohende Wetter, so sagte Hermann, nicht etwa
Schloßen uns bringen und heftigen Guß; denn schön ist die
Ernte.
Und sie freuten sich beide des hohen wankenden Kornes,
Das die Durchschreitenden fast, die hohen Gestalten,
erreichte.
Und es sagte darauf das Mädchen zum leitenden Freunde:
Guter, dem ich zunächst ein freundlich Schicksal verdanke,
Dach und Fach, wenn im Freien so manchem Vertriebnen
der Sturm dräut!
Saget mir jetzt vor allem, und lehret die Eltern mich
kennen,

But one or two of the women restrained them from crying,
commanding:
"Quiet now, children! She's going to town to buy you some candy.
When the stork brought your brother he passed by the candyman's store and 200
Ordered it for you, and soon you will see her again when she
comes with
All those beautiful bags, which are gilded, and filled with the
candy."
So then the children released her, but scarcely Hermann could
bring her
Loose from their friendly embraces, and handkerchiefs
distantly waving.

VIII

MELPOMENE

Hermann and Dorothea

So then the couple departed, westward directing their footsteps,
Where through cumulous clouds the sun intermittently flickered,
Veiling its face, and but rarely flashing its luminous message
Over the fields and the woods, as an awesome omen of thunder.
"May this threatening weather," said Hermann, "not bring
to our acres
Violent downpour or hailstones! For fair is our harvest this season."
Both of them looked with delight upon the undulant grainfields,
Where as they passed, the grain stood almost as high as their shoulders.
Then said the girl to her friend, as he led her along to his
dwelling:
"Friend, it is you, unto whom this beneficent fortune is owing: 10
Shelter and comfort; while storms are menacing many an exile.
Tell me now above all, and teach me to know your good parents;

Denen ich künftig zu dienen von ganzer Seele geneigt bin;
Denn kennt jemand den Herrn, so kann er ihm leichter genug tun,
Wenn er die Dinge bedenkt, die jenem die wichtigsten scheinen,
Und auf die er den Sinn, den festbestimmten, gesetzt hat.
Darum saget mir doch: wie gewinn ich Vater und Mutter?

Und es versetzte dagegen der gute verständige Jüngling:
O, wie geb ich dir recht, du kluges treffliches Mädchen,
Daß du zuvörderst dich nach dem Sinne der Eltern befragest!
Denn so strebt' ich bisher vergebens, dem Vater zu dienen,
Wenn ich der Wirtschaft mich als wie der meinigen annahm,
Früh den Acker und spät und so besorgend den Weinberg.
Meine Mutter befriedigt ich wohl, sie wußt es zu schätzen;
Und so wirst du ihr auch das trefflichste Mädchen erscheinen,
Wenn du das Haus besorgst, als wenn du das deine bedächtest.
Aber dem Vater nicht so; denn dieser liebet den Schein auch.
Gutes Mädchen, halte mich nicht für kalt und gefühllos,
Wenn ich den Vater dir sogleich, der Fremden, enthülle.
Ja, ich schwör es, das erstemal ist's, daß frei mir ein solches
Wort die Zunge verläßt, die nicht zu schwatzen gewohnt ist;
Aber du lockst mir hervor aus der Brust ein jedes Vertrauen.
Einige Zierde verlangt der gute Vater im Leben,
Wünschet äußere Zeichen der Liebe, sowie der Verehrung,
Und er würde vielleicht vom schlechteren Diener befriedigt,
Der dies wüßte zu nutzen, und würde dem besseren gram sein.

Freudig sagte sie drauf, zugleich die schnelleren Schritte
durch den dunkelnden Pfad verdoppelnd mit leichter Bewegung:
Beide zusammen hoff ich fürwahr zufrieden zu stellen;
Denn der Mutter Sinn ist wie mein eigenes Wesen,

Since henceforward my will is to serve them with utter devotion.
For a servant aware of her master more easily gives satisfaction,
When she considers the things which appear to him most
important,
And upon which his mind has been fixed with firmest decision.
So now just tell me how I can win the esteem of your parents."

Hermann replied to the maiden with kindness and full
understanding:
"O, how right is your question, you clever and excellent maiden!
Asking at first about habits and wishes and mind of my parents! 20
Hitherto vain were my efforts to give my father due service.
Though I endeavored to work as if I myself owned the tavern,
Working in vineyard and field from earliest dawn until sunset.
Mother was easy to satisfy: she was aware of my labor.
You will win her regard as the very flower of women,
If you take care of the house as you would of your own
dear possession.
Father is not of this mind: for he loves appearances also.
Good lass: think me not cold, nor devoid of filial affection,
As I describe my father to you, though a stranger, quite frankly.
Never before, I assure you, has any such statement escaped me; 30
Truly my tongue is quite unaccustomed to gossip or chatter,
But you lure from my heart every one of its deepest hid secrets.
Certain refinements of life are a part of my father's requirements.
Outward tokens of love he insists on as well as obeisance.
Even a less satisfactory servant would meet his approval,
Could he but exploit this weakness; while he would frown on
a better."

Joyfully answered the girl, as she gracefully quickened her
foot pace;
(Which was already quite rapid), there on the path in the
gloaming:
"Both of your parents, I hope, will find my work to their liking.
For your mother's manner of thinking strongly resembles 40

Und der äußeren Zierde bin ich von Jugend nicht fremde.
Unsere Nachbarn, die Franken, in ihren früheren Zeiten
Hielten auf Höflichkeit viel; sie war dem Edlen und Bürger
Wie den Bauern gemein, und jeder empfahl sie den Seinen.
Und so brachten bei uns auf deutscher Seite gewöhnlich
Auch die Kinder des Morgens mit Händeküssen und
Knixchen
Segenswünsche den Eltern, und hielten sittlich den Tag aus.
Alles, was ich gelernt und was ich von jung auf gewohnt bin,
Was von Herzen mir geht — ich will es dem Alten erzeigen.
Aber wer sagt mir nunmehr: wie soll ich dir selber
begegnen,
Dir, dem einzigen Sohn, und künftig meinem Gebieter?

Also sprach sie, und eben gelangten sie unter den Birnbaum.
Herrlich glänzte der Mond, der volle, vom Himmel
herunter;
Nacht war's, völlig bedeckt das letzte Schimmern der Sonne.
Und so lagen vor ihnen in Massen gegeneinander,
Lichter, hell wie der Tag, und Schatten dunkeler Nächte.
Und es hörte die Frage, die freundliche, gern in dem
Schatten
Hermann, des herrlichen Baums, am Orte, der ihm so
lieb war,
Der noch heute die Tränen um seine Vertriebne gesehen.
Und indem sie sich nieder ein wenig zu ruhen gesetzet,
Sagte der liebende Jüngling, die Hand des Mädchens
ergreifend:
Laß dein Herz dir es sagen, und folg ihm frei nur in allem.
Aber er wagte kein weiteres Wort, so sehr auch die Stunde
Günstig war; er fürchtete, nur ein Nein zu ereilen,
Ach, und er fühlte den Ring am Finger, das schmerzliche
Zeichen.
Also saßen sie still und schweigend nebeneinander;
Aber das Mädchen begann und sagte: Wie find ich des
Mondes

Mine; and from childhood till now I have known external refinements.
Our former neighbors, the French, in an earlier, happier era,
Treasured courtesy truly: peasant, and noble, and townsman
Had this virtue in common, and made it the rule in their families.
Likewise with us on the German side of the border the children
Brought to their parents each morning a kiss of the hand and a curtsy,
Wishing them blessings; and so they would practice good manners till nightfall.
All I have learned from training and habit at home with my parents,
All that comes from my heart, I am ready to show to your father.
Now, who will tell me, however, in just what manner to treat you, 50
You, my future employer, and only son of the household?"

Thus she spoke; at that moment they came to the peartree together.
Brilliantly shone the moon in splendid fulness from heaven;
Night had come as they spoke, and had hidden the glow of the sunset.
There lay before them shadows and lights in conglomerate masses,
Shadows dark as the night, and light as bright as the sunshine.
Hermann listened with joy to her friendly, intelligent query,
There in the shade of the tree where only that day he'd been weeping,
When he spoke with his mother about his beloved Dorothea.
Here they sat down a moment to rest, and lovingly Hermann 60
Took the hand of the maiden, and tenderly gave her his answer:
"Trust but your heart, and follow it freely wherever it leads you."
No further word did he venture, though this was a favorable moment:
Great was his fear to elicit only a hasty refusal.
Also he felt on her finger the ring, a doleful reminder.
Thus they sat there reposing in silence beside one another,
Till Dorothea observed: "I think the moonlight is lovely:

Herrlichen Schein so süß! er ist der Klarheit des Tags gleich.
Seh ich doch dort in der Stadt die Häuser deutlich und Höfe,
An dem Giebel ein Fenster; mich deucht, ich zähle die
Scheiben.

Was du siehst, versetzte darauf der gehaltene Jüngling,
Das ist unsere Wohnung, in die ich nieder dich führe,
Und dies Fenster dort ist meines Zimmers im Dache,
Das vielleicht das deine nun wird; wir verändern im Hause.
Diese Felder sind unser, sie reifen zur morgenden Ernte.
Hier im Schatten wollen wir ruhn und des Mahles genießen.
Aber laß uns nunmehr hinab durch Weinberg und Garten
Steigen; denn sieh, es rückt das schwere Gewitter herüber,
Wetterleuchtend und bald verschlingend den lieblichen
Vollmond.
Und so standen sie auf und wandelten nieder, das Feld hin,
Durch das mächtige Korn, der nächtlichen Klarheit sich
freuend;
Und sie waren zum Weinberg gelangt und traten ins Dunkel.

Und so leitet' er sie die vielen Platten hinunter,
Die, unbehauen gelegt, als Stufen dienten im Laubgang.
Langsam schritt sie hinab, auf seinen Schultern die Hände;
Und mit schwankenden Lichtern, durchs Laub, überblickte
der Mond sie,
Eh er, von Wetterwolken umhüllt, im Dunkeln das Paar ließ.
Sorglich stützte der Starke das Mädchen, das über ihn
herhing;
Aber sie, unkundig des Steigs und der roheren Stufen,
Fehlte tretend, es knackte der Fuß, sie drohte zu fallen.
Eilig streckte gewandt der sinnige Jüngling den Arm aus,
Hielt empor die Geliebte; sie sank ihm leis auf die Schulter,
Brust war gesenkt an Brust und Wang an Wange.
So stand er,
Starr wie ein Marmorbild, vom ernsten Willen gebändigt,

Splendid its radiant glow, and bright almost as the daytime.
Clearly I see in the village the houses and courtyards all gleaming;
There in the gable a window: its panes are so clear I could count them." 70

"What you see there," said Hermann, with patience restraining his ardor,
"Happens to be where my parents reside, and there we are going.
My room is under the gable, the one whose window you noticed.
Now it well may be yours: we are planning numerous changes.
These fields also are ours: we hope to harvest tomorrow.
Here in the shade we will rest and enjoy a harvesters' dinner.
Come now: let us quickly go down through the vineyard and garden.
See where the ominous storm is moving closer and closer.
Lightning is flashing, and black clouds darken the glow of the moonlight."
So then they rose, and, quickening their steps, walked down through the grainfield, 80
Through the flourishing stalks, rejoicing in nocturnal brilliance.
So they arrived at the vineyard and entered the shadowy darkness.

Down the numerous flagstones Hermann led Dorothea.
These, set unhewn in position, served as steps for the arbor.
Slowly she walked down behind him, her hands holding firmly his shoulders;
Flick'ring through foliage and branches, the moon looked pensive upon them,
Till, enwrapped in a cloudbank, it left the couple in darkness.
Carefully Hermann stepped and gave support to the maiden.
She, not knowing the path, nor the flagstones' faulty condition,
Missed a step as she walked; her ankle gave way, and she stumbled. 90
Quickly the thoughtful young fellow extended his arm to support her;
Lifted up his beloved, who gently leaned on his shoulder.
Breast reclined upon breast, and cheek upon cheek. Thus he stood there,
Fixed as a statue of marble, controlled by his firmness of purpose;

Drückte nicht fester sie an, er stemmte sich gegen die
Schwere.
Und so fühlt' er die herrliche Last, die Wärme des Herzens,
Und den Balsam des Atems, an seinen Lippen verhauchet,
Trug mit Mannesgefühl die Heldengröße des Weibes.

Doch sie verhehlte den Schmerz, und sagte die
scherzenden Worte:
Das bedeutet Verdruß, so sagen bedenkliche Leute,
Wenn beim Eintritt ins Haus, nicht fern von der Schwelle,
der Fuß knackt.
Hätt ich mir doch fürwahr ein besseres Zeichen gewünschet!
Laß uns ein wenig verweilen, damit dich die Eltern nicht
tadeln
Wegen der hinkenden Magd, und ein schlechter Wirt du
erscheinest.

IX

URANIA

Aussicht

Musen, die ihr so gern die herzliche Liebe begünstigt,
Auf dem Wege bisher den trefflichen Jüngling geleitet,
An die Brust ihm das Mädchen noch vor der Verlobung
gedrückt habt:
Helfet auch ferner den Bund des lieblichen Paares vollenden,
Teilet die Wolken sogleich, die über ihr Glück sich
heraufziehn!
Aber saget vor allem, was jetzt im Hause geschiehet.

Ungeduldig betrat die Mutter zum drittenmal wieder
Schon das Zimmer der Männer, das sorglich erst sie
verlassen,

Braced to support the weight of her person, he pressed her
no closer.
Thus he sensed the magnificent burden, the warmth of her
heartbeat,
Sensed, quite close to his lips, her breathing's fragrant aroma;
Held, with a feeling of manhood, the majestic form of the woman.

Yet she concealed her discomfort and said, in a jocular manner:
"This foretells complication, as wise old people have told me: 100
When, as one enters a house, he stumbles, close to the threshold.
I, to be sure, would have wished a more auspicious prognostic!
Let us delay here a moment; your parents then will not chide you,
Saying, 'The maid is lame, and you are a thoughtless provider!' "

IX

URANIA

Prospect

Muses, who joyfully favor the heartfelt affection of lovers,
Who, in guiding this splendid young man, and directing his
footsteps,
Even before his engagement have brought his beloved to his bosom,
Help to unite more completely this winsome and lovely
young couple;
Scatter the clouds, we beseech you, which threaten to shadow
their rapture!
Now, if it please you, reveal whatever indoors has happened.

Filled with impatience, the mother entered again for a third
time
Into the room where the men were, having just anxiously left it,

Sprechend vom nahen Gewitter, vom schnellen Verdunkeln
des Mondes;
Dann vom Außenbleiben des Sohns und der Nächte
Gefahren;
Tadelte lebhaft die Freunde, daß, ohne das Mädchen zu
sprechen,
Ohne zu werben für ihn, sie so bald sich vom Jüngling
getrennet.
Mache nicht schlimmer das Übel! versetzt' unmutig der
Vater;
Denn du siehst, wir harren ja selbst, und warten des
Ausgangs.

Aber gelassen begann der Nachbar sitzend zu sprechen:
Immer verdank ich es doch in solch unruhiger Stunde
Meinem seligen Vater, der mir, als Knaben, die Wurzel
Aller Ungeduld ausriß, daß auch kein Fäschen zurück blieb
Und ich erwarten lernte sogleich, wie keiner der Weisen.
Sagt, versetzte der Pfarrer, welch Kunststück brauchte
der Alte?
Das erzähl ich euch gern, denn jeder kann es sich merken,
Sagte der Nachbar darauf. Als Knabe stand ich am Sonntag
Ungeduldig einmal, die Kutsche begierig erwartend,
Die uns sollte hinaus zum Brunnen führen der Linden.
Doch sie kam nicht; ich lief, wie ein Wiesel, dahin und
dorthin,
Treppen hinauf und hinab, und von dem Fenster zur Türe.
Meine Hände prickelten mir; ich kratzte die Tische,
Trappelte stampfend herum, und nahe war mir das Weinen.
Alles sah der gelassene Mann; doch als ich es endlich
Gar zu töricht betrieb, ergriff er mich ruhig beim Arme,
Führte zum Fenster mich hin, und sprach die bedenklichen
Worte:
Siehst du des Tischlers da drüben für heute geschlossene
Werkstatt?
Morgen eröffnet er sie; da rühret sich Hobel und Säge,

Spoke of the gathering storm, and the rapid departure of moonlight,
Then of the absence of Hermann, and of the perils of nighttime, 10
Forcefully chiding the envoys for leaving Hermann so quickly,
Not having spoken a word to the girl in behalf of poor Hermann.
"Don't make things worse than they are!" exclaimed her husband in anger,
"We are waiting here also, and are eager to know what has happened."

Calmly, then, as he sat there, the neighbor began a long story:
"I shall ever be thankful, in restless moments of waiting,
To my father departed, who carefully rid me in boyhood
Of my impatience, uprooting every fiber completely.
Then, in a moment, I learned how to wait, far better than wise men."
"Tell us," responded the pastor, "just how did your father contrive it?" 20
"That I'll be happy to tell you, for there's something for everyone in it,"
Answered the neighbor. "One Sunday, when I was no more than a youngster,
Waiting, I stood with impatience, and eagerly looked for the carriage,
Which was supposed to convey us out to the well by the lindens.
But it did not appear, and I ran through the house like a weasel,
Upstairs and downstairs; from the doors to the windows I scrambled.
Pins and needles I felt in my hands, and I scratched all the tables,
Stomping and trampling around, and approaching quite close to crying.
Calmly my father observed me, but when I became too excited,
Taking my arm he quietly brought me close to the window, 30
Spoke then these ominous words: 'Do you see the carpenter's workshop,
There on the other side of the street? It is closed for the Sabbath.
Yet he will open tomorrow, and planes and saws will be working

Und so geht es von frühe bis Abend die fleißigen Stunden.
Aber bedenke dir dies: der Morgen wird künftig erscheinen,
Da der Meister sich regt mit allen seinen Gesellen,
Dir den Sarg zu bereiten und schnell und geschickt zu vollenden;
Und sie tragen das bretterne Haus geschäftig herüber,
Das den Geduldgen zuletzt und den Ungeduldigen aufnimmt,
Und gar bald ein drückendes Dach zu tragen bestimmt ist.
Alles sah ich sogleich im Geiste wirklich geschehen,
Sah die Bretter gefügt und die schwarze Farbe bereitet,
Saß geduldig nunmehr und harrete ruhig der Kutsche.
Rennen andere nun in zweifelhafter Erwartung
Ungebärdig herum, da muß ich des Sarges gedenken.

Lächelnd sagte der Pfarrer: Des Todes rührendes Bild steht,
Nicht als Schrecken dem Weisen, und nicht als Ende dem Frommen.
Jenen drängt es ins Leben zurück, und lehret ihn handeln;
Diesem stärkt es, zu künftigem Heil, im Trübsal die Hoffnung;
Beiden wird zum Leben der Tod. Der Vater mit Unrecht
Hat dem empfindlichen Knaben den Tod im Tode gewiesen.
Zeige man doch dem Jüngling des edel reifenden Alters
Wert, und dem Alter die Jugend, daß beide des ewigen Kreises
Sich erfreuen und so sich Leben im Leben vollende!

Aber die Tür ging auf. Es zeigte das herrliche Paar sich,
Und es erstaunten die Freunde, die liebenden Eltern erstaunten
Über die Bildung der Braut, des Bräutigams Bildung vergleichbar;
Ja, es schien die Türe zu klein, die hohen Gestalten
Einzulassen, die nun zusammen betraten die Schwelle.
Hermann stellte den Eltern sie vor, mit fliegenden Worten.

Constantly, all the day long, from dawn till late in the evening.
Think now, carefully, of this: some time in the future the
morning
Will come when the carpenter's journeymen all will be busy
Getting ready the coffln for *you*; they will skilfully, quickly
Finish that house made of boards, and busily carry it hither,
Destined to hold in the end the restless as well as the patient,
Under a heavy roof, which is soon to be shovelled upon it.' 40
Everything then I imagined at once as he had described it,
Saw the boards being nailed, and the black paint carefully readied;
Patiently therefore I sat and awaited the carriage, not moving.
Now, when everyone else is running about in excitement,
Doubtful of what is to happen, I always remember the coffin."

Smiling the pastor responded: "The moving figure of death
holds
Neither fear for the wise, nor seems like an end to devout men.
Death impels the wise man to life, and inspires him to action;
While the devout man is strengthened, in hope of future salvation,
For to both of them death becomes life. Your father was wrong in 50
Showing a sensitive lad like yourself death's literal meaning.
One should rather explain to the youthful the value of nobly
Ripening age; let youth show their elders that both
can take pleasure
In the perpetual cycle of life, which thus finds fulfillment."

Then of a sudden the door swung wide, and there entered
the splendid
Pair; and the friends were astonished, astonished also the parents,
When they saw that the bride was as tall and well formed as
the bridegroom.
Yes, the door seemed too small to admit them, so great was
their stature,
Now as they crossed the threshold together and entered the parlor.
Hermann presented her then to his parents in great agitation: 60

Hier ist, sagt' er, ein Mädchen, so wie ihr im Hause sie wünschet.
Lieber Vater, empfanget sie gut; sie verdient es. Und liebe
Mutter, befragt sie sogleich nach dem ganzen Umfang der Wirtschaft,
Daß ihr seht, wie sehr sie verdient, euch näher zu werden.
Eilig führt' er darauf den trefflichen Pfarrer beiseite,
Sagte: Würdiger Herr, nun helft mir aus dieser Besorgnis
Schnell, und löset den Knoten, vor dessen Entwicklung ich schaudre.
Denn ich habe das Mädchen als meine Braut nicht geworben,
Sondern sie glaubt, als Magd in das Haus zu gehn, und ich fürchte,
Daß unwillig sie flieht, sobald wir gedenken der Heirat.
Aber entschieden sei es sogleich! Nicht länger im Irrtum
Soll sie bleiben, wie ich nicht länger den Zweifel ertrage.
Eilet und zeiget auch hier die Weisheit, die wir verehren!
Und es wendete sich der Geistliche gleich zur Gesellschaft.
Aber leider getrübt war durch die Rede des Vaters
Schon die Seele des Mädchens; er hatte die munteren Worte,
Mit behaglicher Art, im guten Sinne gesprochen:
Ja, das gefällt mir, mein Kind! Mit Freuden erfahr ich, der Sohn hat
Auch wie der Vater Geschmack, der seiner Zeit es gewiesen,
Immer die Schönste zum Tanze geführt, und endlich die Schönste
In sein Haus, als Frau, sich geholt; das Mütterchen war es.
Denn an der Braut, die der Mann sich erwählt, läßt gleich sich erkennen,
Welches Geistes er ist, und ob er sich eigenen Wert fühlt.
Aber ihr brauchtet wohl auch nur wenig Zeit zur Entschließung?
Denn mich dünket fürwahr, ihm ist so schwer nicht zu folgen.

Hermann hörte die Worte nur flüchtig; ihm bebten die Glieder
Innen, und stille war der ganze Kreis nun auf einmal.

"Here," he said, "is a girl of the sort you will want to have with you.
Father dear, welcome her warmly, for she is deserving and, mother,
Question her narrowly now about her knowledge of housework;
Then you will see how much she deserves to approach you more closely."
Hastily then he plucked at the sleeve of the excellent pastor,
Saying to him: "Reverend sir, please help me now in my trouble;
Quickly untangle this knot, for I am too frightened to do it.
I have not ventured as yet to sue for the hand of the maiden;
She has offered herself as a servant, and I am a-tremble,
Lest, when marriage is mentioned, she turn away in repulsion. 70
Let it be settled at once! She must *not* be deceived any longer.
Neither can I endure the suspense and the torment of waiting.
Hurry then to the rescue; make use of the wisdom we honor."
Promptly the clergyman turned and looked to see what had happened.
But he discovered the girl had been hurt by the words of the father;
Hurt to the quick, though the father had pleasantly spoken;
Kindly, with best of intentions, he spoke to the maiden as follows:
"Yes, I am pleased beyond measure, my child! I am happy to notice
Good taste passing from father to son. I have always possessed it.
Always I brought to the dances the loveliest girl of the village. 80
Finally I married her: you can guess whom I mean—it's my wife there.
For by the wives who are chosen by men it is easy to judge them;
What their intelligence is, and how high their self-estimation.
But, I am sure that *your* decision took only a moment
For, if I say to myself, it is really not hard to accept him."

Hermann hardly could hear what was spoken, so much was he trembling
Inwardly; silence suddenly fell upon everyone present.

Aber das treffliche Mädchen, von solchen spöttischen Worten,
Wie sie ihr schienen, verletzt und tief in der Seele getroffen,
Stand, mit fliegender Röte die Wange bis gegen den Nacken
Übergossen; doch hielt sie sich an und nahm sich zusammen,
Sprach zu dem Alten darauf, nicht völlig die Schmerzen verbergend:
Traun! zu solchem Empfang hat mich der Sohn nicht bereitet,
Der mir des Vaters Art geschildert, des trefflichen Bürgers;
Und ich weiß, ich stehe vor euch, dem gebildeten Manne,
Der sich klug mit jedem beträgt, und gemäß den Personen.
Aber so scheint es, ihr fühlt nicht Mitleid genug mit der Armen,
Die nun die Schwelle betritt und die euch zu dienen bereit ist;
Denn sonst würdet ihr nicht mit bitterem Spotte mir zeigen,
Wie entfernt mein Geschick von eurem Sohn und von euch sei.
Freilich tret ich nur arm, mit kleinem Bündel ins Haus ein,
Das mit allem versehn die frohen Bewohner gewiß macht;
Aber ich kenne mich wohl, und fühle das ganze Verhältnis.
Ist es edel, mich gleich mit solchem Spotte zu treffen,
Der auf der Schwelle beinah mich schon aus dem Hause zurücktreibt?

Bang bewegte sich Hermann, und winkte dem geistlichen Freunde,
Daß er ins Mittel sich schlüge, sogleich zu verscheuchen den Irrtum.
Eilig trat der Kluge heran, und schaute des Mädchens
Stillen Verdruß und gehaltenen Schmerz und Tränen im Auge.
Da befahl ihm sein Geist, nicht gleich die Verwirrung zu lösen,
Sondern vielmehr das bewegte Gemüt zu prüfen des Mädchens.

But the excellent maiden, offended and hurt to the quick by
Mockery (so it indeed seemed to her) stood blushing with anger;
From her cheek to the nape of her neck the crimson was spreading. 90
Yet she retained full control, and gathered her forces together;
Answered the innkeeper then, not entirely concealing her heartache:
"Truly, for such a reception your son by no means prepared me.
He depicted his father to me as an excellent burgher!
Well, I see I am standing before him, this man of refinement,
Who can speak to each one in a manner befitting his station.
But it appears that you feel no compassion for me as I stand here.
Poor as I am, I have crossed your threshold, ready to serve you.
Otherwise how could you speak with such scorn just to show me how distant
Fate has kept me from you and your son and from all your good fortune. 100
Truly, I enter your house with only the smallest of bundles,
Your house, which with its splendor gladdens the hearts of its owners;
But I too am aware of my worth, and I feel my dishonor.
Is it then noble to mock me, just as I enter your household,
Driving me nearly away, when I scarcely have stood in the doorway?"

Anxiously Hermann stepped close to the pastor and motioned that he should
Say something now to dispel the unfortunate misunderstanding.
Quickly the pastor stepped forward and looked at the girl in her trouble,
Saw her silent vexation, the tears in her eyes, and her anguish.
Then he was told by the spirit to stay the problem's solution, 110
So as to test a bit further the maiden's emotional mettle.

Und er sagte darauf zu ihr mit versuchenden Worten:
Sicher, du überlegtest nicht wohl, o Mädchen des Auslands,
Wenn du bei Fremden zu dienen dich allzu eilig entschlossest,
Was es heiße das Haus des gebietenden Herrn zu betreten;
Denn der Handschlag bestimmt das ganze Schicksal des Jahres,
Und gar vieles zu dulden verbindet ein einziges Jawort.
Sind doch nicht das schwerste des Diensts die ermüdenden Wege,
Nicht der bittere Schweiß der ewig drängenden Arbeit;
Denn mit dem Knechte zugleich bemüht sich der tätige Freie:
Aber zu dulden die Laune des Herrn, wenn er ungerecht tadelt,
Oder dieses und jenes begehrt, mit sich selber in Zwiespalt,
Und die Heftigkeit noch der Frauen, die leicht sich erzürnet,
Mit der Kinder roher und übermütiger Unart:
Das ist schwer zu ertragen, und doch die Pflicht zu erfüllen
Ungesäumt und rasch, und selbst nicht mürrisch zu stocken.
Doch du scheinst mir dazu nicht geschickt, da die Scherze des Vaters
Schon dich treffen so tief, und doch nichts gewöhnlicher vorkommt,
Als ein Mädchen zu plagen, daß wohl ihr ein Jüngling gefalle.

Also sprach er. Es fühlte die treffende Rede das Mädchen,
Und sie hielt sich nicht mehr; es zeigten sich ihre Gefühle
Mächtig, es hob sich die Brust, aus der ein Seufzer hervordrang,
Und sie sagte sogleich mit heiß vergossenen Tränen:
O, nie weiß der verständige Mann, der im Schmerz uns zu raten
Denkt, wie wenig sein Wort, das kalte, die Brust zu befreien
Je von dem Leiden vermag, das ein hohes Schicksal uns auflegt.

So he addressed her as follows, with words intended to test her:
"Surely you acted too quickly, O maiden and stranger, agreeing
Quite unreflecting, I fear, when you settled to work here with strangers.
Enter the house of your master, and your fate for a year is decided;
Handshake and word of consent obliges a servant to suffer
Much that is hurtful. Indeed the heaviest burden of service
Is not the wearying footwork, nor even the bitter, remorseless
Sweat of the toil, for the free man actively shares in the tasks of
Servants and maids. Much harder to bear are the whims of the master, 120
Undeserved censure, capricious commands, and uncertain directions,
Wishes about which he is not sure, and quite undecided;
Even the mistress is easily angered and shows you no mercy;
And the children are rough and unmannered and constantly irksome:
All this is hard to endure, and still do your duty unswerving,
Quickly and smilingly, too, and yet never grumble nor slacken.
You seem to me not created to stand such a life, since the father's
Jokes so deeply offend you; yet I know no more common occurrence:
Teasing a girl because a young man has attracted her fancy."

Thus he spoke. And the maiden, who felt how right was his discourse, 130
Now could bear it no longer; her feelings showed themselves strongly,
Swelling her breast with a sigh: she could not restrain it from coming.
So she declared on the instant, shedding hot tears as she said it:
"Even a reasonable man, who plans in our pain to advise us,
Never will know how little his coolness can bring us release from
Sorrows that destiny laid on our lives to suffer forever.

Ihr seid glücklich und froh, wie sollt ein Scherz euch verwunden!
Doch der Krankende fühlt auch schmerzlich die leise Berührung.
Nein; es hülfe mir nichts, wenn selbst mir Verstellung gelänge.
Zeige sich gleich, was später nur tiefere Schmerzen vermehrte
Und mich drängte vielleicht in stillverzehrendes Elend.
Laßt mich wieder hinweg! Ich darf im Hause nicht bleiben;
Ich will fort und gehe, die armen Meinen zu suchen,
Die ich im Unglück verließ, für mich nur das Bessere wählend.
Dies ist mein fester Entschluß; und ich darf euch darum nun bekennen,
Was im Herzen sich sonst wohl Jahre hätte verborgen.
Ja, des Vaters Spott hat tief mich getroffen: nicht, weil ich
Stolz und empfindlich bin, wie es wohl der Magd nicht geziemet,
Sondern weil mir fürwahr im Herzen die Neigung sich regte
Gegen den Jüngling, der heute mir als ein Erretter erschienen.
Denn als er erst auf der Straße mich ließ, so war er mir immer
In Gedanken geblieben; ich dachte des glücklichen Mädchens,
Das er vielleicht schon als Braut im Herzen möchte bewahren.
Und als ich wieder am Brunnen ihn fand, da freut' ich mich seines
Anblicks so sehr, als wär mir der Himmlischen einer erschienen.
Und ich folgt ihm so gern, als nun er zur Magd mich geworben.
Doch mir schmeichelte freilich das Herz (ich will es gestehen)
Auf dem Wege hierher, als könnt ich vielleicht ihn verdienen,
Wenn ich würde des Hauses dereinst unentbehrliche Stütze.
Aber, ach! nun seh ich zuerst die Gefahren, in die ich

You are happy and cheerful, so how should a jest be offensive?
But to a sick man even the slightest of touches is painful.
No! were I able to hide my emotions it nought would avail me.
Let there be visible now what later would deepen my sorrow, 140
Cause me perhaps to remain in this silent and grim desolation.
Let me return whence I came, for here I never can tarry!
Let me go now, to search for those miserable exiles, my people,
Whom in their woe I deserted, and selfishly chose what was better.
This is my firm resolution: so now I may tell you quite frankly
Something which otherwise always I would have kept as a secret.
Yes, the derisive remarks of the father offended me deeply,
Not because I am proud or resentful, as servants should not be;
Quite a different reason impelled me: there stirred in my bosom
Tender affection for him who appeared on this day as my savior; 150
For, when he left me there in the road I could not refrain from
Constantly thinking about him: I thought of the fortunate maiden
Whom in his heart he already probably treasured as promised.
Then, when I found him again at the spring, I rejoiced in his coming;
Happier I would not have been had an angel descended from Heaven;
Gladly I followed him then, when he hired me to serve with his parents.
Yet I flattered myself in my heart—I am free to admit it—
As we were walking together, that still I might hope to deserve him,
If I could ever become the dependable stay of the family.
Now at last I can see how I thoughtlessly plunged into danger, 160

Mich begab, so nah dem still Geliebten zu wohnen.
Nun erst fühl ich, wie weit ein armes Mädchen entfernt ist
Von dem reicheren Jüngling, und wenn sie die
Tüchtigste wäre.
Alles das hab ich gesagt, damit ihr das Herz nicht verkennet,
Das ein Zufall beleidigt, dem ich die Besinnung verdanke.
Denn das mußt ich erwarten, die stillen Wünsche verbergend,
Daß er sich brächte zunächst die Braut zum Hause geführet;
Und wie hätt ich alsdann die heimlichen Schmerzen ertragen!
Glücklich bin ich gewarnt, und glücklich löst das Geheimnis
Von dem Busen sich los, jetzt, da noch das Übel ist heilbar.
Aber das sei nun gesagt. Und nun soll im Hause mich länger
Hier nichts halten, wo ich beschämt und ängstlich nur stehe,
Frei die Neigung bekennend, und jene törichte Hoffnung.
Nicht die Nacht, die breit sich bedeckt mit sinkenden Wolken,
Nicht der rollende Donner (ich hör ihn) soll mich verhindern,
Nicht des Regens Guß, der draußen gewaltsam herabschlägt,
Noch der sausende Sturm. Das hab ich alles ertragen
Auf der traurigen Flucht, und nah am verfolgenden Feinde.
Und ich gehe nun wieder hinaus, wie ich lange gewohnt bin,
Von dem Strudel der Zeit ergriffen, von allem zu scheiden.
Lebet wohl! ich bleibe nicht länger; es ist nun geschehen.

Also sprach sie, sich rasch zurück nach der Türe bewegend,
Unter dem Arm das Bündelchen noch, das sie brachte,
bewahrend.
Aber die Mutter ergriff mit beiden Armen das Mädchen,
Um den Leib sie fassend, und rief verwundert und staunend:
Sag, was bedeutet mir dies? und diese vergebenen Tränen?

Planning to live so close to the man I secretly worshipped.
Now for the first time I feel how remote an impoverished maiden
Is from a wealthy young man, no matter how great be her virtue.
This I have told you, all of it, lest you misjudge my intentions.
Chance words wounded my heart, yet to them I owe my deliv'rance.
What could I hope for, secretly hiding my wishes, except that
Soon he would lead by the hand his wedded wife to his hearthside.
Then I could have endured my secret anguish no longer!
Fortune has warned me in time, and fortune has torn from my bosom
That which I closely had guarded, now while the wound can find healing! 170
This much now have I spoken. Nothing further can hold me
Here in this house, where I stand in disgrace and embarrassed confusion,
Freely admitting my love and the foolish delusion I cherished.
Neither the darkness and lowering clouds which cover the night, nor
Ominous thunder (hear how it rolls!) can prevent me, not even
Tempests of wind and the downpouring deluge can stop me. For I have
Suffered all of these things, in my sorrowful wand'ring and exile,
Whilst I fled from the merciless foe as he closely pursued me.
Now, once again, I depart, in a way that has long been familiar,
Seized by the whirlpool of time, and destined to leave all behind me. 180
Farewell! Longer I will not stay! For now it is finished."

Thus having spoken she rapidly walked to the doorway behind her,
Grasping under her arm the bundle she brought when she entered.
But the mother took hold of the maiden, embracing her firmly,
Holding her fast with both arms, exclaiming amazed and astonished:
"Tell me, just what does this mean? And why do you weep without reason?

Nein, ich lasse dich nicht; du bist mir des Sohnes Verlobte.
Aber der Vater stand mit Widerwillen dagegen,
Auf die Weinende schauend, und sprach die verdrießlichen Worte:
Also das ist mir zuletzt für die höchste Nachsicht geworden,
Daß mir das Unangenehmste geschieht noch zum Schlusse des Tages!
Denn mir ist unleidlicher nichts, als Tränen der Weiber,
Leidenschaftlich Geschrei, das heftig verworren beginnet,
Was mit ein wenig Vernunft sich ließe gemächlicher schlichten.
Mir ist lästig, noch länger dies wunderliche Beginnen
Anzuschauen. Vollendet es selbst; ich gehe zu Bette.
Und er wandte sich schnell, und eilte zur Kammer zu gehen,
Wo ihm das Ehbett stand, und wo er zu ruhen gewohnt war.
Aber ihn hielt der Sohn, und sagte die flehenden Worte:
Vater, eilet nur nicht und zürnt nicht über das Mädchen!
Ich nur habe die Schuld von aller Verwirrung zu tragen,
Die unerwartet der Freund noch durch Verstellung vermehrt hat.
Redet, würdiger Herr! denn euch vertraut ich die Sache.
Häufet nicht Angst und Verdruß; vollendet lieber das Ganze!
Denn ich möchte so hoch euch nicht in Zukunft verehren,
Wenn ihr Schadenfreude nur übt statt herrlicher Weisheit.

Lächelnd versetzte darauf der würdige Pfarrer und sagte:
Welche Klugheit hätte denn wohl das schöne Bekenntnis
Dieser Guten entlockt, und uns enthüllt ihr Gemüte?
Ist nicht die Sorge sogleich dir zur Wonn und Freude geworden?
Rede darum nur selbst! was bedarf es fremder Erklärung?
Nun trat Hermann hervor, und sprach die freundlichen Worte:

No! I will not let you go—for you are my dear son's betrothèd."
But then the father uprose indignant and vexed beyond measure,
Stared at the girl shedding tears, and voiced, before all,
his vexation:
"Well! It is thus you reward me, for all my forbearance and kindness! 190
Now, at the close of the day, unpleasantness rules in my household.
Nothing to me is more hateful than noisy weeping of women,
Passionate outcries that serve to increase the confusion and trouble,
Which, with a little good sense, could be settled in easier
fashion.
I have now had enough of this unreasonable nonsense.
Settle the business yourselves! For me it is long past my bedtime."
Quickly he turned toward the door and started to go to the
bedroom,
Where his marriage bed stood, and where he usually rested.
But his son held him and spoke to him, fondly beseeching his father:
"Father, do not be hasty! and please, do not censure the maiden! 200
I alone am to blame, for I have caused all the confusion,
Which our friend has increased by his unexpected deception.
Speak, your reverence, I beg you; to you I confided my secret.
Do not pile fear on resentment; please, settle the matter forever!
How could I ever revere you in future so highly, if now you
Substitute malice for wisdom, and fail in your noble vocation?"

Smiling, the dignified pastor responded to Hermann's beseeching:
"What other wisdom, indeed, could have drawn this lovely
admission
Straight from the heart of this maiden and thus have displayed
her good nature?
Has not your care in one moment been changed into joy,
into rapture? 210
Speak for yourself! Do not ask someone else to do your explaining!"
Thereupon Hermann stepped forward, and spoke pleasant words
to the maiden:

Laß dich die Tränen nicht reun, noch diese flüchtigen
Schmerzen;
Denn sie vollenden mein Glück und, wie ich wünsche, das
deine.
Nicht das treffliche Mädchen als Magd, die Fremde, zu
dingen,
Kam ich zum Brunnen; ich kam, um deine Liebe zu werben.
Aber, ach! mein schüchterner Blick, er konnte die Neigung
Deines Herzens nicht sehn; nur Freundlichkeit sah er im
Auge,
Als aus dem Spiegel du ihn des ruhigen Brunnens begrüßtest.
Dich ins Haus nur zu führen, es war schon die Hälfte des
Glückes.
Aber nun vollendest du mir's! O, sei mir gesegnet!—
Und es schaute das Mädchen mit tiefer Rührung zum
Jüngling,
Und vermied nicht Umarmung und Kuß, den Gipfel der
Freude,
Wenn sie den Liebenden sind die lang ersehnte Versichrung
Künftigen Glücks im Leben, das nun ein unendliches
scheinet.

Und den übrigen hatte der Pfarrherr alles erkläret.
Aber das Mädchen kam, vor dem Vater sich herzlich mit
Anmut
Neigend, und so ihm die Hand, die zurückgezogene,
küssend,
Sprach: Ihr werdet gerecht der Überraschten verzeihen,
Erst die Tränen des Schmerzes, und nun die Tränen der
Freude.
O, vergebt mir jenes Gefühl! vergebt mir auch dieses,
Und laßt nur mich ins Glück, das neu mir gegönnte, mich
finden!
Ja, der erste Verdruß, an dem ich Verworrene schuld war,
Sei der letzte zugleich! Wozu die Magd sich verpflichtet,
Treu, zu liebendem Dienst, den soll die Tochter euch leisten.

"Have no regret for your tears, nor yet for these fugitive sorrows:
They have perfected my joy, and, I hope, your happiness also.
I did not come to the fountain to hire a maid for our
household;
No, I was seeking the love of a wonderful girl at the fountain.
But my embarrassment kept me from seeing your heart's
inclination;
All I could see in your eyes, as reflected there in the water,
Was, as I thought, but a greeting of courtesy, not of affection.
Half of my happiness then was to bring you here to my family. 220
Now you complete it: God bless you for all the joy you have
given!"
Then, with heartfelt emotion, the maiden looked at her lover,
Welcomed his kiss and embrace, the summit of rapture; for
these are

Pledges for lovers of longed for assurance that joy will continue
All through their lives, which seem to them now to stretch
endless before them.

Soon, for the others, the pastor had clarified all the enigmas.
Then however the girl stepped up to the father, and,
bowing,
Kissed with respectful affection his hand, though he sought to
withdraw it,
Saying, "Dear sir, in justice, you will forgive me, surprised as
I was, first for my sorrowful weeping, and now for
my joyous. 230
Pardon the feelings I showed, and pardon my present emotion.
Let me, I beg you, discover the measure of gladness that
heaven
Just has bestowed on me. Let this first of vexations be also,
Now and forever, the last! For that which your handmaid has
promised,
Namely, affectionate service, will now be performed by your
daughter."

Und der Vater umarmte sie gleich, die Tränen verbergend.
Traulich kam die Mutter herbei und küßte sie herzlich,
Schüttelte Hand in Hand; es schwiegen die weinenden
Frauen.
Eilig faßte darauf der gute verständige Pfarrherr
Erst des Vaters Hand und zog ihm vom Finger den
Trauring,
(Nicht so leicht; er war vom rundlichen Gliede gehalten)
Nahm den Ring der Mutter darauf und verlobte die Kinder;
Sprach: Noch einmal sei der goldenen Reifen Bestimmung,
Fest ein Band zu knüpfen, das völlig gleiche dem alten.
Dieser Jüngling ist tief von der Liebe zum Mädchen
durchdrungen,
Und das Mädchen gesteht, daß auch ihr der Jüngling
erwünscht ist.
Also verlob ich euch hier und segn' euch künftigen Zeiten,
Mit dem Willen der Eltern, und mit dem Zeugnis des
Freundes.

Und es neigte sich gleich mit Segenswünschen der Nachbar.
Aber als der geistliche Herr den goldenen Reif nun
Steckt' an die Hand des Mädchens, erblickt' er den anderen
staunend,
Den schon Hermann zuvor am Brunnen sorglich betrachtet.
Und er sagte darauf mit freundlich scherzenden Worten:
Wie! du verlobest dich schon zum zweitenmal?
Daß nicht der erste
Bräutigam bei dem Altar sich zeige mit hinderndem
Einspruch!
Aber sie sagte darauf: O, laßt mich dieser Erinnrung
Einen Augenblick weihen! Denn wohl verdient sie der Gute,
Der mir ihn scheidend gab und nicht zur Heimat zurückkam.
Alles sah er voraus, als rasch die Liebe der Freiheit,
Als ihn die Lust, im neuen veränderten Wesen zu wirken,
Trieb nach Paris zu gehn, dahin, wo er Kerker und Tod
fand.

Straightway the father embraced her, concealing his tears from the others;
Then the mother approached her and kissed her with hearty affection.
Hand locked in hand, the two women continued their weeping in silence.
Quickly the clergyman then, a man of kindly discernment,
First grasped the hand of the father, and drew the ring from his finger 240
(This was no easy task: for the finger was not of the thinnest),
Then the ring of the mother, and with them affianced the children,
Saying: "Now, once again, let the golden rings serve their function:
Welding a bond as firm as the first one, in every way like it.
This young man is stirred to the depths by his love for the maiden;
Also the girl admits that the youth has all her affection.
So I declare you betrothed, and invoke on your future a blessing,
With the consent of your parents, and the family friend to stand witness."

Straightway the druggist approached, and saluted the couple with blessings.
But when the clergyman put the ring on the hand of the maiden, 250
How astonished he was to behold on her finger another
Ring, which Hermann had anxiously noticed before at the fountain.
And he said thereupon with jocular friendly amazement:
"What, you were plighted before? And this is your second betrothal?
What if your first fiancé at the altar raises objection?"
But she responded to this: "O let me devote but a moment
To this remembrance. Indeed, such a good man amply deserves it.
Parting, he gave me this ring, and never returned to his homeland.
For he foresaw what would happen, and soon his devotion to freedom,
And his desire to be active and useful where change was occurring 260
Drove him to Paris, where prison and death were his fortune.

Lebe glücklich, sagt'er. Ich gehe; denn alles bewegt sich
Jetzt auf Erden einmal, es scheint sich alles zu trennen.
Grundgesetze lösen sich auf der festesten Staaten,
Und es löst der Besitz sich los vom alten Besitzer,
Freund sich los von Freund: so löst sich Liebe von Liebe.
Ich verlasse dich hier; und, wo ich jemals dich wieder
Finde—wer weiß es? Vielleicht sind diese Gespräche die
letzten.
Nur ein Fremdling, sagt man mit Recht, ist der Mensch hier
auf Erden;
Mehr ein Fremdling als jemals, ist nun ein jeder geworden.
Uns gehört der Boden nicht mehr; es wandern die Schätze;
Gold und Silber schmilzt aus den alten heiligen Formen;
Alles regt sich, als wollte die Welt, die gestaltete, rückwärts
Lösen in Chaos und Nacht sich auf, und neu sich gestalten.
Du bewahrst mir dein Herz; und finden dereinst wir uns
wieder
Über den Trümmern der Welt, so sind wir erneute
Geschöpfe,
Umgebildet und frei und unabhängig vom Schicksal.
Denn was fesselte den, der solche Tage durchlebt hat!
Aber soll es nicht sein, daß je wir, aus diesen Gefahren
Glücklich entronnen, uns einst mit Freuden wieder
umfangen,
O, so erhalte mein schwebendes Bild vor deinen Gedanken,
Daß du mit gleichem Mute zu Glück und Unglück bereit
seist!
Locket neue Wohnung dich an und neue Verbindung,
So genieße mit Dank, was dann dir das Schicksal bereitet.
Liebe die Liebenden rein, und halte dem Guten dich dankbar.
Aber dann auch setze nur leicht den beweglichen Fuß auf;
Denn es lauert der doppelte Schmerz des neuen Verlustes.
Heilig sei dir der Tag; doch schätze das Leben nicht höher
Als ein anderes Gut, und alle Güter sind trüglich.
Also sprach er: und nie erschien der Edle mir wieder.
Alles verlor ich indes, und tausendmal dacht ich der
Warnung.

'Live, and be happy,' he said. 'I am going, for all is in ferment
Now in the world, and everything seems to be near dissolution.
Laws of firmly established governments now are a-crumbling;
Property now is sequestered from legally authorized owners;
Friends are leaving their friends, and loved ones leaving their
loved ones.
Here I must leave you too, and when or where I will find you
No one can tell us, for this may well be our last conversation.
Man is a stranger on earth, so they say, and say rightly, and now as
Never before in our time we are strangers one to another. 270
Ours is the earth no longer—our treasures are fast disappearing;
Gold and silver are melted out of the ancient and holy
Patterns; everything is in motion; the world we had fashioned
Seems to desire dissolution in night and in chaos; it craves a
New birth: you will be faithful to me, and if we should ever
Meet one another again beyond the world's desolation,
Then we shall be like persons renewed and transformed and no
longer
Bound to our fate, for what could control the survivors of chaos?
But if it be not permitted that, once escaped from these dangers,
We may embrace each other again with joy in the future, 280
Then, I beg you, do keep in your thoughts my soaring example;
Face with unwavering heart the prospect of grief or of gladness.
If you are tempted to form a new union or seek a new dwelling,
Gratefully take and enjoy whatever your destiny offers.
Love those sincerely who love you; respond to those who act
kindly;
Walk on the pathway of life with care not to stumble or falter;
Twice as much anguish awaits you, if ever your loss is repeated.
Holy be all your days! Yet think not that life is more precious
Than any other possession: possessions can always deceive you.'
Thus spoke this noble young man, and never again did I 290
see him.
All that I had, I have lost, and his warning has echoed a
thousand

Nun auch denk ich des Worts, da schön mir die Liebe das Glück hier
Neu bereitet und mir die herrlichsten Hoffnungen aufschließt.
O, verzeih, mein trefflicher Freund, daß ich, selbst an dem Arm dich
Haltend, bebe! So scheint dem endlich gelandeten Schiffer
Auch der sicherste Grund des festesten Bodens zu schwanken.

Also sprach sie, und steckte die Ringe nebeneinander.
Aber der Bräutigam sprach, mit edler männlicher Rührung:
Desto fester sei, bei der allgemeinen Erschüttrung,
Dorothea, der Bund! Wir wollen halten und dauern,
Fest uns halten und fest der schönen Güter Besitztum.
Denn der Mensch, der zur schwankenden Zeit auch schwankend gesinnt ist,
Der vermehret das Übel, und breitet es weiter und weiter;
Aber wer fest auf dem Sinne beharrt, der bildet die Welt sich.
Nicht dem Deutschen geziemt es, die fürchterliche Bewegung
Fortzuleiten, und auch zu wanken hierhin und dorthin.
Dies ist unser! so laß uns sagen und so es behaupten!
Denn es werden noch stets die entschlossenen Völker gepriesen,
Die für Gott und Gesetz, für Eltern, Weiber und Kinder
Stritten und gegen den Feind zusammenstehend erlagen.
Du bist mein; und nun ist das meine meiner als jemals.
Nicht mit Kummer will ich's bewahren und sorgend genießen,
Sondern mit Mut und Kraft. Und drohen diesmal die Feinde,
Oder künftig, so rüste mich selbst und reiche die Waffen.
Weiß ich durch dich nur versorgt das Haus und die liebenden Eltern,
O, so stellt sich die Brust dem Feinde sicher entgegen.
Und gedächte jeder wie ich, so stünde die Macht auf
Gegen die Macht, und wir erfreuten uns alle des Friedens.

Times in my heart, and I think of it now, when the fortune of love brings
Happiness fairly before me, and opens up splendid new vistas.
Pardon, dear friend, that even while holding your arm I must tremble.
Thus to a sailor whose life has been saved in a storm it seems always,
Even on firmest of shores, as though the ground were unstable."

Thus having spoken she settled the ring on top of the other.
But then the bridegroom spoke out, and said, with manly emotion:
"All the more firmly let us establish, amid the upheaval,
Dear Dorothea, our union. Let us preserve and maintain it, 300
Holding fast to each other, and to our lovely possessions.
One who is apt to be changeable, now in this changeable epoch,
Causes the evil to prosper, and spreads it further and further.
But a man firm of resolve can shape his world to his liking.
Germans should never desire to continue this terrible movement,
Nor is it fitting for them to waver this way and that way.
This land is ours! Thus should we speak, and thus should maintain it.
Resolute peoples indeed have always deserved commendation,
When they have striven for God and for law, for parents and wives and
Children, and, standing together, have fallen in hostile encounter. 310
You are mine: now that which is mine is mine more than ever.
I will not keep it in sorrow nor mar its enjoyment by worry.
I will use my courage and strength. Should enemies threaten
Now or in future, get my equipment and hand me my weapons.
For, can I only be sure that you are protecting my house and
Parents, who love me, I fear not to stand in mine enemies' presence.
Strength would rise against strength if everyone shared my opinion,
And on us all the blessings of peace would descend in abundance."